D1436537

TO THE UNKNOWN GOD

TO THE UNKNOWN GOD

Essays towards a Religion

by

JOHN MIDDLETON MURRY

*

Jonathan Cape Ltd

THIRTY BEDFORD SQUARE LONDON

FIRST PUBLISHED IN MCMXXIV
SECOND IMPRESSION MCMXXX

PRINTED IN GREAT BRITAIN BY
BUTLER & TANNER LTD
FROME

Contents

Preface

ALL THESE ESSAYS SAVE ONE ORIGinally appeared in *The Adelphi*, and the remaining one, on 'Literature and Religion,' would have appeared in those small pages had it not been too long for them. They have, I believe, a certain unity of thought and intention, though I do not know how to define it more closely than by saying that they represent the effort of a man of thirty-four to take stock, as honestly as he could, of his attitude to life, conscious and unconscious, formulated and unformulable. 'As honestly as he *could*,' I say, because one of the few things I have learned is that it is very hard to be honest. One's capacity for self-deception is almost infinite. I have done my best to be honest: that is all I claim. That it was my best in that direction is proved, to my own satisfaction at least, by the fact that when I settled to the work of revising these essays, I found there was very little in them I could honestly change.

I have mitigated a few hasty expressions and expanded others that were too summary: but substantially they remain as I wrote them month by month. The essay 'Literature and Religion' is only a more detailed, some might say a more philosophic, statement of the position in which I find myself. I have also included, by the author's permission, a criticism of my attitude towards Christianity and the Church by Dr. W. E. Orchard. It seemed to me necessary that this should be included if only to explain the controversial element in some of the essays.

I should also have liked to include an attack on my attitude as a whole made by Mr. Alan Porter of *The Spectator*. Unfortunately he refused permission.

Though one of these critics is friendly, the other hostile, they are in essential agreement on their main count against me. It is that I am an individualist, a rebel against authority, a despiser of tradition.

That I am an individualist, I admit: that I am a rebel against authority and a despiser of tradition I emphatically deny. Because I do not accept the same authority and claim the same tradition as they do, it does not follow that I accept no authority and claim no tradition. Far from it. The underlying theme of these essays, the philosophic and religious background implicit in them (and at times, I had believed, explicit also) is that individualism itself is a high tradition, and that in this tradition are contained universal authorities. I sincerely believe that I accept these authorities and follow the tradition which they compose.

What my critics apparently find hard to understand, or to forgive if they do understand, is that the

process of discovering this tradition and accepting
these authorities of mine, has been in the main a process of self-exploration. I have accepted nothing
that I have not comprehended. I have come to comprehend things which ten years ago, five years ago, I
should have thought it impossible for myself to comprehend; I have found in myself faculties of knowledge of which in times past I had no suspicion; I
have come to be certain that the most important kind
of knowledge is 'not rational, neither is it irrational';
and it may be that as the years go on I shall come to
comprehend and know more than I do now. But
the process of that further understanding, if it is
granted me, will be governed by the same law that
has governed the process up till now. The law is
that I can accept the sentence of no man and no body
of men, until it is corroborated by my own knowledge and ratified by my own experience. My
authorities will always be the authorities I cannot
help accepting, because some secret comprehension
insists that they are true; my tradition will always be
the tradition to which I discover that I have always
belonged—that of the soul *nullius addictus jurare in
verba magistri*.

One of my critics vehemently accuses me of vanity.
I have re-read these essays carefully, and find myself
in this respect at least unconscious of sin. But that
is for others to judge. It is hard to know oneself, and

although I think I know from personal experience what vanity is, it may be that I unconsciously display vanity in these pages. But if, as I suspect, my critic discerns vanity in my resolution to stand or fall by my own certitudes, I reply that this is not vanity at all. It is simply one man's way of reaching a truth by which he can live. It seems to me that I have had no choice in this matter: I was made what I am by powers over which I have had no real control; I was destined to be one of those who cannot take things on trust, who have to know for themselves. And, I admit, I find it hard to understand those who are unlike me in this respect. I have to know that a thing is wrong before I can believe it is wrong; I have to know that a thing is true before I can believe it is true.

It is simply because I believe that there are many others essentially like me, whose experience has yet been different from mine (as it must needs have been), that I have put down as honestly as I could, month by month, my thoughts and beliefs. I have known what it is to discover in the records of a man before me the sudden evidence that he had passed through a situation like my own, and the comfort of the instant knowledge that one is, after all, not wholly isolated, not altogether queer; and it has seemed to me that for the privilege of giving another a moment of this knowledge, a grain of this comfort, it was worth while to risk the disapprobation and downright hostility of those who seem never to have passed through the deserts of loneliness and despair. It was for these unknown members of the tradition to which I belong that the magazine in which these essays appeared was chiefly founded, and for them that they were written. I wanted them at least to have an inkling of what I had discovered – above all, of this, that they were not wholly isolated either now or through the ages, but that there was a long sequence of great men, to whom the world pays lip-service, who had passed through doubts and desolation of the same kind as theirs, only more grievous, and attained to comprehension at the last.

I make no claim at all to a knowledge of any final truth. I have, in spite of Mr. Porter's persuasion to the contrary, no desire to prophesy for the sake of prophesying. I have only desired to declare my belief that at the end of the path of a sincere individualism comprehension will be found; that if this path is followed honestly, as an acceptance of obligations, not falsely as a satisfaction of caprice, it does not end in the sterility of rebellion, in which indeed, as Ivan Karamazov said, a man can hardly live, but in a knowledge and a security which are abiding. To this knowledge and security I do not pretend, but that it can be achieved is proved to me beyond all doubt by the example of the heroes of the past who have been compelled to take this way, and who form the tradition I try to follow and the authorities I accept. By the nature of the enterprise it is impossible that I should have given in these essays more than a faint indication of what is to be found in these men and their works. That would be, and I hope will be, the labour of a lifetime.

Finally, in my effort to revise these essays, I have been constantly confronted by the fact that they were written for the rather peculiar magazine in which they appeared. *The Adelphi* is woven into their very texture in such a way that the attempt to eliminate it would make their fabric threadbare. This seemed at first to be an insuperable difficulty: on second thoughts it appeared to be merely an inevitable condition of their being published at all. They would not have been published at all except in *The Adelphi*: except for *The Adelphi* they would never have been written. To eliminate *The Adelphi* from them would be as foolish as to cut out a man's backbone and expect him to live.

(*July*, 1924).

The Cause of it All

NOWADAYS I ONCE MORE RIDE ON the top of a 'bus from Trafalgar Square to Hampstead. It is a favourite ride of mine; it has always had the merit of taking me home. Suddenly I look down over the side at the crowd of people on the pavement corner at Camden Town, and I am astonished and frightened. Not always. Nine days out of ten I can do this thing with impunity. I look, but I do not see. But on the tenth something happens. I am aware of a dozen people rushing violently, as though possessed, towards the *Star* man's yellow poster. The Thousand Guineas! And I, who have drawn a blank in every sweepstake for which I paid my half-crown, who once went as a schoolboy to the City and Suburban and stood for an hour watching a bookmaker called "Fred Bacon of Putney" — he drank a bottle of Bass regularly at five-minute intervals — without daring to hand him the shilling I wanted to gamble, realize that I understand nothing about people at all.

The top of my 'bus becomes as the firm deck of a ship in an unknown ocean. For a moment the mere thought that I might have to descend into that crowd appals me. I am frightened. I say to myself that if I were really to get down, it would be all right. I have only to stop one of the men so blindly intent on learning the winner of the four-o'clock race, to ask him the way to some street or other, and he will treat me like a human being and a brother. For a second he may even forget that he wants to know the winner, while he repeats: 'Third to the right, second to the left, under the arch by the cabman's shelter — that'll take you *right* into it.' He will stop to say it even a third time. I shall find it, in fact, quite hard to get away.

So it would be, I know, and so I argue myself out of my unreasoning fear. We are very much the same sort of people. If he were to ask *me* the way, I should find myself also repeating for the third time: 'Third to the right, second to the left . . .' and he might find it hard to get away from *my* civility. Yes, indeed, it's hard to choose between us. He cannot get through a day without the excitement of putting a shilling on a horse; I cannot get through one without the excitement of wondering what it is all about. That is precisely what I was wondering when I took that ill-advised glance down on to the pavement at Camden Town. It was that which made me feel that there was a gulf between us. If I had told him my thought, he would have smiled compassionately. Now, I see that if he had told me the winner of the four-o'clock race, I should have found nothing better to do than to smile compassionately also.

That is comforting. We are in the same boat, after

all. And perhaps we are after very much the same kind of thing. He seeks satisfaction for his soul in backing horses, I in wondering what men live by nowadays. His betting and my preoccupation are cousins at least. The chief difference between us, I suppose, is that his particular kind of drug, like insulin, needs to be injected every twenty-four hours, except on Sunday when there is the *News of the World*, while I keep myself going by looking for something whose effect shall be permanent.

That is enough to go on with. I no longer have the feeling that I may be engaged in something futile and incomprehensible. I confess that it did seize hold of me. When I began to write these first few words of a new magazine, I was suddenly smitten with the terror that visited me when I glanced down on the crowd at Camden Town. There is a gulf between us: why make the vain attempt to bridge it? It was all very well (said my attendant demon) when you were occupied in trying to get *The Adelphi* organized. Then you ran from printer to paper-maker, from paper-maker to estate agent, and when you got home you passed the remaining hours in writing letters. You had no time to think about what you were doing. You were caught up in the practical business of realizing an idea you had months ago. But now that self-forgetful phase is over. You are up against it, chuckled my demon.

Furthermore, he whispered to me of the happiness I had thrown away — the full sight of the perfection of that spring I had waited for, when, as each February day brought still more rain, I said to myself: But how wonderful this May will be! I have not seen it. A spring that was precious to me beyond all other springs I have simply thrown away, in order to stump up and down the pavements of Fleet Street and the Adelphi. There never will be such another spring as this one I have rejected; there never can be. When I went back, the other day, to the remote cottage I lived in through February and March, the apple trees were in full bloom. The place was changed; I had not even seen the buds begin to open; I had lost touch. I had promised myself that not a day should pass without my going to learn — something I needed to learn — from watching each apple tree come into its own. Yet I should not have returned to the cottage at all had it not contained a manuscript I needed for this magazine!

During these weeks of activity, when I have been editor, press-agent, advertising man, and business manager rolled into one, I have had no time to think at all. I have only known my demon was waiting for me the moment I had time to turn my head his way.

To-night he caught me. I must have known it was going to happen. After hoarding up this evening, setting it apart days ahead, for the purpose of writing this introductory article, I suddenly said to my friends friends who were going to a dinner-party, 'I'll come with you.' I don't like dinner-parties. After long experience I have come to the conclusion that they are not in my line. I systematically elude them. Yet to-night I positively jumped at the chance of going to a dinner-party to which I had not even been invited.

Not because I am afraid of work. I have done as much work as most people, and indeed I rather like it. But simply because I was afraid of my demon. Afraid unconsciously, of course. If I had known I was trying to avoid him, I would have done my utmost to look him in the eyes. I have found it the best way.

As it was, I had got so far as beginning to change my clothes before I knew I was shirking. Then I put my coat on again, and on my way downstairs to a solitary supper, called out, 'No, I'm not coming after all. I've got to work.' There was some argument; but I held my ground. The door slammed with an empty echo.

Then, in the silent house, the trouble began. I felt very much alone. Well, that had happened before: I know how to deal with that. But I had to do something more, to begin to write, to justify what I was doing, to write boldly, to unfurl and wave a flag. And my demon simply sniggered. What *is* the point? he said. What *can* you do? And then he gave up questions and played his trump cards. He recalled my glimpse from the 'bus at Camden Town; he put my garden before me in all its beauty. It was clever of him; but he has lost the game.

No, when it comes to the point, the secret, deep-down point that sometimes takes years to discover, we know we are not isolated. That is enough. But we can say more. We believe in life. Just that. And to reach that belief, to hold it firm and unshakable, has been no easy matter for some of us. We have paid for it.

But now we have it, we know it is a precious thing. We have to fight for it. We know it is worth fighting for, the only thing worth fighting for. We fight in our own way with our pens. But what we write with our pens will have been paid for, honestly, by our lives, in the world of experience.

To fight, for people like ourselves, means to make sacrifices. You will meet with many names you know in this magazine. Probably you will buy it because you have learned to trust in one or other of them. But each one of these people whose name is familiar to you will have made a sacrifice by writing for *The Adelphi*.

But don't run away with the idea that this magazine is run by charity. 'You will live either by charity or advertisement,' Mr. Bernard Shaw wrote at the end of a prospectus which I sent him. But there are some things which Mr. Bernard Shaw does not care to know. He is a clever man, infinitely more clever than I am; and yet I know one or two things that he does not know, because he does not want to know them. One of these is that there is such a thing as disinterested enthusiasm for an idea. Perhaps *The Adelphi* will prove it to him.

At present Mr. Shaw believes that I am 'an energetic young journalist who has succeeded in persuading a capitalist to part with enough money to set him up as editor of a magazine.' It's so plausible that even I had my moment of doubt. 'Journalist' – yes, of course. 'Young' – thirty-four isn't exactly old. 'Energetic' – well, in a way. 'Succeeds in persuading a capitalist' – the little that there is was offered unasked, by a friend to a friend. Still, as near to the truth as most statements are. And yet all wrong, utterly and hopelessly wrong.

This magazine is run neither by capital nor by charity nor by advertisement, but by a belief in life. I have not cajoled a single person to write for it. I have put the idea before them as straightforwardly as I could; and I have waited for the answer. I have told you part of Mr. Shaw's. The rest are secret; but I am content.

For lack of words I have been inaccurate. Belief in life is not, strictly speaking, an idea at all. It is a

faith. A moment comes in a man's life when suddenly all the hard things are made plain, when he
knows quite simply that there is a good and a bad,
that he must fight for the one and make war on the
other. And the good things are the things which
make for life, and the bad things are the things which
make for decay. He begins to know which is which.
Not with his head, that poor old head which has
landed him in so many quagmires, led him into so
many dazes and mazes, but with some faculty far
simpler, far more living, far more exacting in its
demands upon his loyalty than the mere intellect can
ever be. And now what was an inclination becomes a
necessity, what was a distaste becomes a hatred, what
was a possibility becomes a passion.

I do not mean that all those who will write in *The
Adelphi* believe in life in my way. Some of them do,
I know; and some of them reached their belief before
me. There is a generation which has had to struggle
for a faith; there is an older generation which was not
involved in that necessity. Perhaps these two generations can never quite understand each other. It does
not matter. There is something better than understanding. There is this instant recognition that in
spite of all differences and peculiarities we are on the
same side – together for life, together against decay.
That is good enough. We can ask for nothing more,
for nothing better.

But don't go away with the notion that we shall be a tuneful and harmonious choir of the young and the old and the middle-aged, chanting incessant Hosannas to Life. There are, as I say, different ways, many different ways, of believing in life. I think I can recognize them when I see them; but I should be hard put to it to invent a neat little intellectual definition to include them all. But here are some of them. You may simply believe that life, as it is, squalor lit by sudden splendours, splendour darkened by sudden squalors, is in itself glorious and enchanting and beautiful. Or you may believe that life as it is is terrible, a mere caricature of the splendid thing it might be. Or may you believe that the truth is precious and the lie is hateful beyond all other earthly things we know. Or you may believe that literature and music and painting at their pinnacle reveal to us Pisgah sights of a mode of existence more perfect and more candid than our own, a world we might inhabit, if only our minds would suddenly slip sideways across the thin abyss. Or you may believe that man has it in his power, if only he had the will, so to reshape his own inward being that mood and circumstance have no more dominion over him. Or you may believe that the serene world of science, that keen compulsive air in which the lie collapses instantly by its own rottenness, is the tabernacle of the Lord where man should delight to dwell for ever.

Any of these things, and other things like these, you may believe in, and by believing in them you will believe in life, *if* — —. If you believe in them passionately, if you are prepared to make sacrifices for them, if, when the moment comes, you are prepared to *act* on their behalf.

The Adelphi is nothing if it is not an act. It is not a business proposition, or a literary enterprise, or a nice little book in a pretty yellow cover; it is primarily and essentially an assertion of a faith that may be held in a thousand different ways, of a faith that life is important, and that more life should be man's chief endeavour; that the writers who give us life, the men of science who seek to make our knowledge and command of it more central, and all those who try to express by the written word their conviction that man's conduct of life is his most pressing concern, are knit together by a common conviction that man must be true to his own experience.

Perhaps that is the secret, vague though the phrase may be. For there is the experience which comes from without, and the reaction to that experience which comes from within. Yet both are experience. To have learned through enthusiasms and sorrows what things they are within and without the self that make for more life or less, for fruitfulness or sterility; to hold to the one and eschew the other; to seek to persuade and reveal and convince; to be ready to readjuſt one's values at the summons of a new truth that is known and felt; to be unweary in learning how to discriminate more sharply between the false and the true, the trivial and the significant, in life and in men and in works; to be prepared to take a risk for what seems the finer and better thing — that is, perhaps, all we can do. Yet somehow, as I write the words, that 'perhaps all we can do' seems a very meagre phrase. The endeavour to be true to experience ſtrikes me at this moment as the moſt precious privilege of all. To have found a loyalty from which one cannot escape, which one muſt for ever acknowledge — no, one cannot ask for more.

All this, I know, is the moſt frightful give-way. Above all for an editor. But I am not an editor. I would do anything, I verily believe, rather than be an editor any more. Anyone who can do the job whose scope I have been trying to describe may have my place for the asking; and I will help to pay his salary, because I believe that now, at this point of time, it has got to be done. Till he comes forward I will hold the fort. But I am only a *locum tenens* for a better man.

So I am quite undiſturbed by the thought that I have given myself away. I really don't care a rap for the clever ones and the sniggerers and the people who say 'How amusing!' because they haven't anything truer to say. Once upon a time I was rather frightened of them. But now no more. I know that there are important things – and they are not among them. Except in so far as they corrupt the atmosphere.

Besides, it is as well that I should have given myself away pretty completely. First, because I don't want people to buy this magazine under false pretences. I want them to have an inkling of the kind of thing they may expect to find in it. All I ask is that if occasionally they get a shock, they should wait a day or two and try to make up their minds whether it may not, after all, have been a salutary and life-giving shock, before they stop their order at the newsagent's.

The second reason why I am glad to have given myself away is that, as I see it in my mind's eye, this magazine will be the place where other and more important people than myself will give themselves away. When a man expresses his deepest convictions he cannot help giving himself away with both hands. And now is the time when those who have convictions must make their voices heard above the chatter of those who have none.

24

Mr. Joiner and the Bible

I AM NOT VERY ELOQUENT IN LIT-
erary (or in any other) discussion. Unless my man
knows me and I know him well, my spasmodic irrele-
vances slowly sink into utter silence. I can present
my case far better to a blank sheet of paper than to
the blank visage of a human being. And more often
than not I go away to chew the cud of retrospection
and to indulge in an orgy of what the best people call
l'esprit d'escalier.

The other day I fell into such a debate. 'I have
now reached a point,' said my opponent, 'where I
am interested only in the literature which aims at
exerting power, at influencing men's actions.' Since
he happened to be a man whose words do directly
influence men's actions, I could understand him well.
Were I in the same case, I should doubtless be of the
same persuasion. But I am not; so I went my way
ruminating home.

On my way I remembered that quite recently Mr.
H. G. Wells, being asked to name the twelve most
important books, deliberately defined them as the
twelve books which have had the most powerful and
most visible influence on the lives of men. That was
wise of him. Those twelve most important books
have a way of keeping you awake of nights, unless
you hobble the nightmare with a definition. Mr.

Wells, having pegged him down, was able to go blithely and properly on with the making of his list: the Bible, the Koran, the sayings of Confucius, and the rest. At which Mr. W. J. Turner, of the *New Statesman*, was so angry that he forgot he was supposed to be writing musical criticism, and, after quoting a paragraph of Mr. Wells, almost foamed at the mouth. 'What indescribable drivel!' he cried. That was rash of him. First, because 'indescribable' is a dangerous word for a critic to use. If it *is* drivel, he ought to know how to describe it. That is just his business as a critic. Secondly—and more seriously—because Mr. Wells simply does not write 'indescribable drivel.' He may have committed many offences, but that is not one of them. To say that anything of his is 'indescribable drivel' is to be found guilty of describable drivel oneself.

Mr. Turner's feelings ran away with him. But why? What was there to be annoyed about? His behaviour might almost have suggested that Mr. Wells's statement was true, and that it had proved too painful to the *amour propre* of a poet and a musician. Poets probably think that poets ought to have power. And yet, though I myself have written poetry, I am not so sure of this. Certainly, if they had, we should have to be a little more drastic with bad poets than we are. Instead of putting them in anthologies, we should be putting them in gaol.

At all events, the common opinion of mankind to-day is that poets are pretty harmless people, even when they happen to be musical critics as well.

But that does not dispose of the question. Since Mr. Turner was unfortunately made incoherent by his indignation, we must invent somebody else to take his place. . . . He is invented. His name is Mr. Joiner. He is a quiet little man with a slight stammer when he is in unfamiliar company; he wears pince-nez and green Harris tweeds; and he is a member of the minor Civil Service. He reads *The Adelphi*. *The Adelphi*, in fact, is written for Mr. Joiner, because he is one of the people worth writing for. Mr. Joiner reads Shakespeare; he also reads Wells; he goes to the Beethoven Fridays at the Queen's Hall. I have an idea it was he who borrowed from me Trotter's *Instincts of the Herd in Peace and War*. He has grey eyes, nondescript, non-committal eyes. His favourite books are *The Oxford Book of English Verse* and *Our Mutual Friend*, but he also likes *Tristram Shandy*, the more so, oddly enough, because he reached the age of twenty-six before he knew what the first chapter was really about. But Mr. Joiner has got married himself since then. His wife is still pretty, though she is fatter than you would have expected her to be if you had known her, as I did, when she first met Joiner at the Prom. Her name is Rosie. In fact, Mr.

Joiner read H. G. Wells's article to Rosie after Saturday night supper.

'What I like about Wells is,' said Mr. Joiner when he had finished, 'he makes you think.'

Rosie tried to assume the look of one who has been made to think. She frowned for a moment, then decided she didn't want to be wrinkled before her time, and began to put the plates together instead.

'Never thought of it that way before,' said Mr. Joiner.

'Nor did I,' said Rosie, truthfully. 'Never!' And to avert the danger of having to say something that was not so true, she retired with the tray to the scullery. She didn't even ask Joiner to help her with the washing-up.

In fact, she was pleased that Joiner should remain alone, just then.

So Joiner sat in an arm-chair thinking. That red-brick Roman Catholic Church they were building at the end of Edith Road — the Bible did that, he supposed. But did it really? He'd heard that R.C.s didn't give much for the Bible. Neither did anybody else, for the matter of that, as far as he could see. There was that fellow Britwell, who chucked up his job in Somerset House, to go and be a missionary in China. That was a silly thing to do, seeing that Giles's book on China made you feel that China didn't need much in the way of missionaries. If Britwell had been a doctor, a medical missionary, there might have been more sense in it. But then he'd got religion. Mr. Joiner never could understand a man getting religion. Hard-faced men most of them were, too, or they had a sort of breezy sloppiness like that young curate who called from St Agatha's.

No, he couldn't see that the Bible counted for very much nowadays. In the Middle Ages, though. . . . Mr. Joiner had time to bask in a sudden, splendid, and scarlet vision of himself, with bell, book, and candle, excommunicating M. Poincaré for daring to march into the Ruhr, before he suddenly remembered that in those days no one could read the Bible at all. Jolly good things, translations!

Still, you couldn't get rid of the Bible quite so easily. He'd read somewhere that more copies of the Bible were sold every year than all the rest of the books put together. That was a bit exaggerated: must be. But it must have a tremendous circulation. Queer thing Northcliffe didn't get hold of it. A Bible with ads.– pages and pages of ads.! Funny Northcliffe never thought of that. Perhaps he did. Perhaps there was a law against it. Blasphemy? *Lèse Majesté?* No, that wasn't a crime in England. High treason? Mr. Joiner vaguely remembered a Royal coat of arms on the title-page. He hunted among his books to make sure. Not that he really expected to find a Bible among them. But he felt he ought to act as though it might be! They had one somewhere about; he'd seen it somewhere lately. A Sunday-school prize it was. He wondered where it could be.

'Rosie!' he called.

Rosie emerged from the kitchen, wiping her hands upon a towel.

'You don't happen to know where the Bible is?'

'The Bible!'

'It's all right, dear, I haven't got religion. I just want to have a look at it – if you know where it is.'

'It's in the bedroom.'

Mr. Joiner was suspicious.

'Do you read it?' he asked.

'Sometimes,' she said, reluctantly. 'When I'm waiting for you. It's a nice book to read in bed. You can begin anywhere. You don't mind, do you?'

'Good Lord, no! Jolly good book. One of the very best. Diddn't you hear Wells saying so?'

Rosie had not heard. She never did hear what Mr. Joiner read to her. Without replying she ran upstairs. While she was gone, Mr. Joiner's thoughts were inquisitive. When she handed him the book,

'What bits do you read most, darling?' he asked.

'Oh, all sorts—about Benjamin, and David and Jonathan, and Jesus and the little children, and there's the Prodigal Son. I like that best,' she said.

'You don't mind if I borrow it – only for a minute or two?'

30

At the door of the parlour Mr. Joiner turned. 'Rosie!' he called. 'You might find me that bit about the Prodigal Son.' She found it for him.

Mr. Joiner sat back in his arm-chair. He heard Rosie climb the ſtairs, and the sound was sweet to him. It always had been, ever since they came to an underſtanding; but to-night somehow sweeter than before. Then he looked at the title-page. *Cum Privilegio Regis* — By Privilege of the King. That explained it. A jolly good job, too. A Bible with ads. didn't bear thinking about, somehow. Then he began to read the Prodigal Son. He read it twice, and a third time. And for the third time there was a great tug at his heart when he reached the words of the elder son: —

'Lo, these many years do I serve thee, neither transgressed I at any time thy commandment: and yet thou never gaveſt me a kid, that I might make merry with my friends. But as soon as this thy son was come, which hath devoured thy living with harlots, thou haſt killed for him the fatted calf.'

And he said unto him, 'Son, thou art ever with me and all that I have is thine. It was meet that we should make merry and be glad: for this thy brother was dead, and is alive again; and was loſt, and is found.'

Queer thing, that. It got you somehow; simply got you.

There had been other things which 'got' Mr. Joiner. In Shakespeare, principally. When they 'got' him, they stuck in his mind. So now he began to say softly to himself: —

'And whether we shall meet again I know not.
Therefore our everlasting farewell take.
For ever and for ever, farewell, Cassius!
If we do meet again, why, we shall smile;
If not, why then this parting was well made.'

Yes, there was the tug at his heart again. Those noble Romans could do it. The thought brought back yet other lines — strangely precious these, a secret treasure of his, about which no one knew, not even Rosie.

'Our lamp is spent, it's out. Good sirs, take heart!
We'll bury him; and then what's brave, what's noble,
We'll do it after the high Roman fashion
And make death proud to take us.'

'And make death proud to take us,' Mr. Joiner repeated. And, as always before, when he had said it to himself, as he had said it so often, on his way to his chief's room at the office, a sudden thrill shot through his spine. No, he did not care what happened. His very backbone was proud. Let them sack him! He possessed something that could never be taken away.

'The Bible and Shakespeare, Shakespeare and the Bible,' he murmured. 'It's the same sort of thing.'

And then, as he turned out the gas, he felt that it was a wonder and a miracle, no less, that he was going to bed, to sleep with the woman he loved. What more could he ask? Only this, he thought: that they two might also die together.

'And make death proud to take us,' he said to himself, as he climbed the stair.

Then when he had got into bed beside Rosie, he took her, half-asleep into his arms. 'That's a wonderful story, darling,' he whispered. 'That about the Prodigal Son. Then he kissed her as he had not kissed her for years.

A Month After

IT'S A QUEER BUSINESS. A MONTH ago when I sat down to write for *The Adelphi*, I was afraid. And I told you the story. I was afraid that I might be speaking into a void, and that no answer would come save the echo of my own voice. I overcame that fear, and I have told you how – as much, that is, as ever can be told in words. I suddenly knew that what I was doing was worth doing, that it was worth making sacrifices for. What I did not know was that it would succeed. And I had reached a point where I was past caring.

I wanted *The Adelphi* to succeed, of course. But what I wanted far more was that this one job at least of the many I have attempted in my life should be cleanly done. I must not wobble or waver; I must not compromise. Not this time. I had so to do the work, so to write, that when I am called to my account I could say: Yes, I have told many lies, yielded to many fears, whispered applause of things I hated, and joined in laughing at things I love. But there came a moment when there was a risk to be taken, and I took it; when there was something true to be said, and I said it; when I had to have faith in life, in my fellow-creatures, and in my friends, and I found it. That, and that alone, was what I wanted at the last.

And, desiring that with all my heart, I had no thought of success or failure. When the first number of *The Adelphi* went to press I had reached a point where I did not care what people thought of it. That, sounds heroic and exaggerated. I do exaggerate, and I am not a hero. But this is true. I did not care what people thought of it. I had deliberately and once for all given myself away. What I had exposed I could not conceal again. The thing was irrevocable; it could not be otherwise. This, take it all in all, is what I stand for, what in some way or another I am. It is past change, beyond all remedy. I was not elated. I was not depressed. Something that had to be had been.

And then, after a little space, I was told that *The Adelphi* was selling: that it would have to be reprinted. Then, that it must be reprinted again, and then again, until it had reached a number three times as great as I had thought possible in the days when I still revolved the question of success or failure. 'It's gone with a *bang*.' The voice of the business manager (there is one now) seemed to explode over the telephone. The explosion shook me. I began to be afraid once more. And I am still afraid.

Afraid of what? Afraid of many things—but of one above all others. Afraid, first and foremost, that I have created an expectation I cannot fulfil. I am not afraid of the man who writes to me, asking, 'What

do you mean by Life? Define it.' I have no definitions to give. I am tired of definitions, tired of the
people who define poetry and cannot feel it, truth,
and have not a grain of it in their hearts, love, and
have never been touched by it. *The Adelphi* is not
meant for them. If they really and truly want to
know what I mean by life let them read the magazine, and read it again, until they catch with their
being the tone that will for ever elude their minds.
No, I am not afraid of them. But I am afraid of
the simple people who write to me – people to
whom a shilling is precious – to express their
gratitude. I am afraid of the woman who writes this
to me from Plymouth : –

'I feel constrained to write you this letter at once,
just in order to say "Thank you."
'Alone in a strange town, in the throes of a great
bereavement, having come straight from the death-
bed in the accident ward of a public hospital of a
greatly loved friend, smitten down under tragic circumstances in the prime of life, I wandered into a
public library and opened *Public Opinion* on the
arresting headline of your article in *The Adelphi* :
"This magazine is run by a belief in life." It came
to me in my stunned condition like a direct message,
and thrilled me. After days and nights of strenuous
nursing only ending in defeat, I was overwhelmed

with a sense of the uselessness of this terrible battle for a mere existence. The shadow would not lift. Then I read your article and realized that, after all, I do believe in life, though I thought I did not, and that ideals and aspirations are indeed spiritual potencies that here and hereafter demand our loyalty.

'This little note is penned in the library, and is not intended for publication unless you should wish to use it, but it comes straight from my heart.'

I do not want to *use* that letter. But it helps me to explain my fear. I am afraid lest I should fail such people as she, or such as the man who wrote me this: —

'I do not know whether I should congratulate you or not for *The Adelphi*. Somehow your advertisement had caught my soul — "Deals with the problems of life in its own way." Well, I was, and am still, troubled by this terrible enigma — life. I had tried in my way to satisfy my soul; but, alas! what is my way? It had made me more miserable and unhappy. On the 28th I wandered the whole afternoon from newsagent to newsagent to get a copy of *The Adelphi*. No, most of them hadn't heard of it; some yes, they were expecting it. In one little red shop in Charing Cross Road I was told, "It will come to-morrow, not to-day. We have just heard from the publishers." With heavy heart I wandered — wandered aimlessly.

37

Why? I don't know. Somehow or other the ideal of *The Adelphi* had got hold of me, and I was like a moth, determined to whirl round and round the candle till I had either burnt my wings or understood the nature of light.

'Yes, I got it to-day afternoon, read it through — from cover to cover, including the advertisements. Deals with problems of life! In its own way! Alas! what about me? No, I was not disillusioned, I did not expect the impossible from *The Adelphi*. It is all right. As good as it can be in its own way. But I? Am I a rap better now? Has it helped me?'

The writer bursts into a wail of disappointment and disillusion. Life is meaningless and incomprehensible, he cries, and the words of the wise are empty and unprofitable. Then he breaks off again:

'Sir, pardon me. When I took my pen to write I did not know I should make such a mess of my beautiful ideas — scientifically arranged — for I am a student of science. But, well, life will have what it wants, and we have to pay the price. Here I end. Forgive me if you find me a fool — for I am one, and that with a capital F. And remember that I am only twenty-one — and one who used his lunch money to buy Dostoevsky and Tchehov and Tolstoy and Shaw and Gorky; and when one finds, well — and when one uses one's exam. time to read them, and then to

38

ſtir the whole soul and to feel wretched and miserable — it is hopeless. I give it up. I shan't copy this,
nor shall I type it, because I don't mind if you read
it or not. Better throw it in the rubbish-basket.

'But send I will — and if you care to tell me anything
I shall buy your July issue. Farewell till then, for my
head is hot and feverish.'

What shall I say? Say something I muſt. But how to
say something that shall convince? Is it ſtrange that
I am afraid?

To the science ſtudent's queſtion there is no *answer*.
Yet it is answered in all the great literature and great
music and great art of the world. It is great literature
and great music and great art because it holds an
answer to that queſtion. But to learn to read great
literature and to hear great music and to see great
art may be the work of a lifetime. And at twenty-
one? Shall I say then, Read *Antony and Cleopatra* till
the bugle-call of that unearthly challenge to human
loyalty echoes in the remoteſt chamber of the soul?
Or, Liſten to the laſt piano sonatas of Beethoven, till
you feel that in the high B of op. 109 all that human
desire can imagine of the cryſtalline perfection of the
ideal is cracked and shattered, *muſt* be cracked and
shattered, with a faint, far-away sound of breaking
that ſtabs the very quick of being; till you know that
Beethoven faced this disaster, pressed its inevita-

bility home against his heart, and saw what lay beyond
and triumphed and was free? Or shall I say, Read
Tchehov's *The Cherry Orchard*. Read and listen, till
you know what secret harmony and high design lies
within all human discomfiture, to be discovered only
by those who feel, and feeling, do not turn their face
away.

These men, and other men like these, knew the
secret of life. They fought for it and conquered.
Listen to them. Learn to listen to them. Learn to
wait for the silence which descends when the importunate mind grows weary of asking its unanswerable
questions, and to discern what echoes are awakened
in that stillness by the notes which these men plucked
out of their souls. Learn to live by that music,
earthly and divine, or even learn only to desire to
live by it, and you also will triumph and be free.

Ah, but this is hard and obscure. I do not know.
Obscure? There are moments, nowadays, when it
seems to me the simplest thing of all. Hard? Yes, a
knowledge for which you have to pay; which, when
you have paid for it, it is not easy to be true to — but
harder still to betray.

But yet, even now, I have not answered my student
of science. He is twenty-one. I am thirty-four.
Thirteen more years of life. Is that a title to prophesy
to him? Have I a secret in my keeping? Again, I do
not know. But this I do know. The days when I,

too, agonized as he does now are over. I have learned
to accept. But what I mean by acceptance would take
me many hours and many pages to make plain. But,
chief of all, it means this: that my little personality,
which in the old days I so jealously guarded against
the menace of the immensities, does not matter any
more. I am not a whole; I am a part — a tiny and insignificant part may be. I shall do my work as a
part, and when my work is over, I shall go. And
there is no menace in the immensities any more.
Somehow, they have me in their keeping, and —
stranger still — I them in mine. I bear them up, they
me.

One day — or one night rather — I knew this. And
I will try to tell you how. Not many months ago I
lost someone whom it was impossible for me to lose
— the only person on this earth who understood me
or whom I understood. This impossible thing happened. Katherine Mansfield died. For a fortnight I
lived in a dream. Then I awoke. I was alone. But
absolutely alone, as perhaps only a man who has
known what it is to be not alone can know loneliness.
And suddenly I knew that all the friends whom I
loved were nothing to me. If they spoke to me, I
watched their lips form words that had no meaning.
It was as though an empty shell made signs to an
empty shell.

I began to be aware that there was something I must

do. At first it was simply that I must go away. Then it hardened and became clearer: I must *be* alone. Not merely have loneliness thrust on me by the high gods, as it had been, but achieve and perfect it in myself and by myself. And then, knowing this, I was terribly afraid. I remember as I rode along in the January twilight to the solitary cottage I had chosen, at every turn in the misty road I felt a new and a greater fear. It was too much: I was not strong enough for this. And only the still greater fear of returning to the horror of that meaningless converse with my friends kept me from turning back.

Then in the dark, in the dead, still house, I sat at the table facing the fire. I sat there motionless for hours, while I tried to face the truth that I was alone. As I had wanted to turn back, so now I longed to turn away. There was in me something that simply would not look, and, again and again, as it turned its eyes away, I took its head in my two hands and held its face towards what I had to see. Slowly and with an effort I made myself conscious that I was physically alone. Prompted by some instinct, I tried to force this consciousness into every part of my body. Slowly I succeeded. At last I had the sensation that I *was* in my hands and feet, that where they ended I also ended, as at a frontier of my being, and beyond that frontier stretched out the vast immensi-

ties, of space, of the universe, of the illimitable,
something that was other than I. Where I ended,
it began — other, strange, terrible, menacing. It did
not know me, would never acknowledge me, denied
me utterly. Yet out upon this, from the fragile rampart of my own body, I found the courage to peer,
to glance, at last to gaze steadily. And I became
aware of myself as a little island against whose slen-
der shores a cold, dark, boundless ocean lapped de-
vouring. Somehow, in that moment, I knew I had
reached a pinnacle of personal being. I was I, as I
had never been before — and never should be again.

It is strange that I should have known that. But
then I did know it, and it was not strange.

What happened then? If I could tell you that
I should tell you a secret indeed. But a moment came
when the darkness of that ocean changed to light,
the cold to warmth; when it swept in one great wave
over the shores and frontiers of my self; when it
bathed me and I was renewed; when the room was
filled with a presence, and I knew I was not alone —
that I never could be alone any more, that the universe beyond held no menace, for I was part of it,
that in some way for which I had sought in vain so
many years, I *belonged*, and because I belonged, I
was no longer I, but something different, which
could never be afraid in the old ways, or cowardly
with the old cowardice. And the love I had lost was

still mine, but now more durable, being knit into the very substance of the universe I had feared. And the friends whose words had been so meaningless were bound to me, and I to them, for ever. And if it should prove that I had a work to do, or a part to play, I should no longer draw back at the last.

I am very much the same sort of person to look at. I carry the same little bag; I always leave my razor-strop behind; I am always in terror of losing trains, and always catch them breathless with a minute and a-half to spare; I am just as hopeless in dealing with the mechanism of life as ever I was, just as tongue-tied at dinner-parties; I have the same odd dreams of happiness. I don't suppose that even my friends notice any difference. Nevertheless, the difference is there. It is that which enables me to write things like this — which six months ago I could not have written at all. Certainly it is this which made me feel that, no matter what should come of it, I must give the student of science the truest reply I had in me to give. This I have done.

(June, 1923.)

Going Out and Going In

I SELDOM GO OUT TO THE THEATRE.
Indeed, when I come to think of it, I seldom go
out at all. I much prefer to go in. And when I do go
out, I think I have wasted my time unless it has given
me the chance of going in, of fetching out from its
dim hiding-place something precious that I have forgotten or never knew I had. The converse of friends
can do this for me, or rather can help me to do this.
They give me a kind of courage of discovery; they
ask me a question in a voice which says, 'Yes, you
have the answer,' so quietly, with such certainty,
that I too begin to believe I may have it somewhere.
So I take my candle down, light it in the fire of their
confidence, and set off boldly into the disused rooms.
And the marvel i that sometimes I do find something. I bring it out into the light of day. I blink,
I rub it gingerly upon my sleeve. 'Can that be
mine?' I wonder. Indeed, I never cease from wondering this, even when my friends have accepted it
and I have put it in my pocket for my own. But
mine or not, I am the richer for it.

A going-out, for me, must have a going-in for its
reward. Perhaps it is because I am afraid of being
disappointed that I so seldom go out to the theatre.
Yet I have been very fortunate. Of the four plays I
have been out to see in the last three years, two were

miraculous and one made me laugh as I laugh at Pickwick or at the opening of Bealby. That was *Le Médecin malgré lui* at the Odéon laſt spring. The other two were Tchehov's *The Cherry Orchard*, not very well played by the Stage Society, and a matinée produ&ion of *Othello* by Matheson Lang and Arthur Bourchier. This sounds, I fear, as though I were very cultured. I cannot help it. Those are the fa&s. Another fa& is that I wept warm tears when both those plays were ended. Here was my allegiance; this my loyalty. This vision of life was true. There was no more room for regret or sorrow.

> 'Come, come, no time for lamentation now,
>   Nor much more cause.'

No cause, no cause at all. In this enchantment I also had my place; for this moment I too could look on the created world and see that it was good. And when the great Othello turned—

> 'And say besides that in Aleppo once,
>   Where a malignant and a turban'd Turk
>   Beat a Venetian and traduced the State,
>   I took by the throat the circumcised dog
>   And smote his *thus*—

then I discovered in myself a spirit equal to his own and knew what high descent was in my blood.

And when I laughed at *Le Médecin malgré lui*, again

46

I entered into possession of something in myself I had forgotten. Once more, *I did not care*. I was not a hero, I was not wise perhaps as I was wise when I listened to Carlotta's falsetto 'I don't even know whether I *had* a father' on the garden seat in the cherry orchard, but likewise I did not care. The world was full of foolishness and I could laugh; of beauty and I could weep; of greatness and I could breathe. And this time with no penny candle from my own cupboard, but with a great lamp lit by genius, I entered into possession of my own forgotten aptitudes. My going-out had been the prelude to a triumphant going-in. 'We be three Calendars, the sons of kings.'

I suppose it is because I have tasted these things and cannot lightly risk a disappointment that I so seldom go out to the theatre. But the other night I did. I had been told, told many times, that I must see *At Mrs. Beam's*, and since I was told it by one who shares my conviction that Charlie Chaplin is the greatest actor in the world, I inclined my ear. He did not say that *At Mrs. Beam's* was as good as *The Immigrant* or *Easy Street*, for he has a sense of values and knows that such a statement would be incredible. But the mere fact that he could mention a modern English comedy within a breath or two of Chaplin's masterpieces was enough. On the first opportunity I would go.

47

I went. I paid eight and sixpence. I laughed. I could not see what the second act was for. At the rest I laughed. Once, at the scene over the card-table, I laughed a great deal. But never for a single moment did I forget that I had paid eight-and-six for the opportunity. I imagine that I got for my money one sixpenny laugh, two twopenny ones, and about a dozen penny and half-penny ones mixed. One and sevenpence. And it cost me eightpence to get there, and two and ninepence for my dinner out. Debit: one and tenpence and an evening. Credit: one little problem. After all, I did laugh. Probably, if they were measured by the cachinnometer, my laughs were as many as *Le Médecin malgré lui* or *Pay Day* had compelled from me. But those laughs have nothing whatever to do with each other; they would not recognize each other in the street. One bubbles up from my vitals, takes hold of me like an atavism, and I am possessed. The other is just a trick of my physical body. It laughs, and I – I am thinking that a writer is expected to give a great deal better value for eight-and-six than the author of a modern play.

Now those two laughs begin to worry me. I have not settled with them; and I love, above all else, to have settled with things—even with bills, when I can afford it. What is it that makes the difference? What *is* it?

Then I begin to grope for the truth with vague

phrases. The true comic attitude is adequate to life; it is comprehensive, it is profound. Very likely. But it will not do. I must find out more. When Aristophanes guys Socrates, when Falstaff pulls the leg of the world, when the long gamekeeper muses over Mr. Winkle's marksmanship, when Charlie Chaplin converted takes the offertory-box out of his trousers, when Gogol's Tchitchikov appears, entering the provincial town of N.

'In the chaise sat a gentleman, not handsome but not bad-looking, not too stout and not too thin; it could not be said that he was old, neither could he be described as extremely young. His arrival in the town created no sensation whatever, and was not accompanied by anything remarkable —'

when things like this begin to happen, something begins to happen to me. I feel that through these spectacles I could look at the world for ever: by their queer magic all the pain and cruelty of things would be blotted out.

And yet, I wonder. Is that really what I feel? No, it is something subtler. Before many moments are gone, I find myself, even while I laugh, feeling sorry for Mr. Winkle, terrified lest Charlie Chaplin should not escape from the hooligan, full of fears lest the rogue Tchitchikov should be publicly disgraced, and — strangest of all, perhaps—really apprehensive for

Sir John Falstaff. He is running it too fine with the Lord Chief Justice; he will be shut up in the Tower; he will have his head cut off. And when people say, 'What an artistic blunder to make Falstaff a pathetic figure at the last!' I feel that Shakespeare knew what he was about. I suspect that Falstaff is supremely comic because the possibility of disaster is always hanging about him. He is rollicking along a tight-rope. So it is with Tchitchikov; so with Charlie Chaplin, so with Bealby, so with Sganarelle. We are on their side. They are playing single-handed against the machine, against that order to which we have succumbed. They represent all that is rebellious and untamed and living in ourselves. They lie, they cheat, they steal, they do everything except inflict pain, and we applaud them from our hearts. We know that they have need of every pebble they can lay their hands on to sling against their Goliath. They have not the remotest chance of killing him. The most they can hope to do is throw a handful of dust in his eyes, or trip him up with a string, while they run for their little lives. Is a man to stick to Queensberry rules when he is fighting the scheme of things? The truly comic character cannot be a man of honour; he would merely be a fool.

Is not this perhaps the clue to the mystery? The secret of comic laughter is the liberation of some vital spontaneity of act and word from all the mechanisms of control. We give, we long to give, the comic genius and his characters a licence to kick this prim and boring world of ours about, to put carpet-tacks in the seat of authority, and banana-skins in the paths of the planets – and we rush, when once it is started, to join in the game. And that anguished fear that the world, the authorities, and the planets may get their own back – is not that an essential part of the fascination and of the cause why we surrender ourselves with such hysterical abandon to comic laughter when the chance of it comes our way? We snatch at this chance of freedom. And the comic genius himself seems to snatch at it. He feels, perhaps more than we do, that the shades of the prison-house are closing fast. Few comic geniuses have remained comic for long. Shakespeare dropped it suddenly; so did Dickens; Gogol could not keep it up even through a single book – he took a fright that carried him eventually to his death-bed. Perhaps Charlie Chaplin – But no, the thought is too appalling. In a generation which has been brought up in the war as within the walls of a gaol, he alone has been able to escape and throw stones at the windows. There have been months, I verily believe, when he has done more than any living man to keep the soul of humanity alive. If he were to succumb, those many tiny ones who do not read Shakespeare or Dickens or Gogol, but who sit on the threepenny benches and jump in their seats and shriek 'Good old Charlie!' the moment the hat and the trousers and the stick and the moustache wobble into sight, might never learn to laugh at all. But there is no cause for alarm. A new Chaplin film is promised for August. Then, sure that the dormant rebel against the whole sorry scheme of things will be waked in me, sure, that is to say, of my reward of going-in — then, and not till then, I shall go out again.

(June, 1923).

WE LIVE IN WORLDS OF OUR OWN. For long times – days, weeks, months – we may believe that our world is shared by others; that others judge as we judge, imagine as we imagine, respond as we respond, that the same things jar and the same things delight their hearts as ours. We are inveterate optimists – or is it that we have an invincible fear of ultimate loneliness? – and we make haste towards the comfort of believing that truth is as universally current as a Treasury Note, and sincerity as apparent to all men as the Pole Star.

Of course, it is a foolish way of going on; there is no excuse for it, unless as an expression of our invincible faith in a millennium. Experience—wise old nurse to whom we never listen—is quite positive about its foolishness. She tells us we are heading for the crash. Our ears are deaf to her warnings; we go blindly on. The lover still persuades himself that the thought of the beloved is as his own, until one day she utters, in the voice of intimate comprehension that is itself the evidence that no misunderstanding between *them* could ever be, an enormity the more enormous because she does not know it is one. Baudelaire, Tchehov, Katherine Mansfield – each has written an immortal story upon this theme. It is quintessential; that is why they chose it

'Es ist eine alte Geschichte,
        Doch bleibt sie immer neu.'

And it came, with all the shock of novelty, though I
have been through it a thousand times in a thousand
disguises, to me the other day. It began by my re-
ceiving a letter from the Westminster Catholic Association protesting against the essay by Mr. D. H.
Lawrence on 'Education and Sex.' The conclusion
of the essay, said the letter, was a studied insult to the
Christian religion; it passed the comprehension of the
Association how the editor of a responsible review
could have allowed it to appear. As Shakespeare said
– and nobody quite knows what he meant – it was a
cooling card. It would have been positively glacial
had it not come from an Association. But for some
odd reason I can never take associations, federations,
leagues, committees, societies, academies, and other
bodies corporate quite seriously. They are so deper-
sonalized that they seem to lose half the quality of
real existence. So that I had some difficulty in
restraining myself from replying simply that *The
Adelphi* was not a responsible review. For indeed
it is not, if that upholstered phrase means what it
seems in practice to mean. A 'responsible review' –
as far as my experience goes – is one that takes
care not to offend anybody; and the only way to
offend nobody is to be nothing and to say nothing.

In which the 'responsible review' is generally successful.

However, I did not make this reply to the Association. I simply said that if I had thought Mr. Lawrence's article contained a studied insult to Christianity I would not have printed it. No sooner had I sent the answer than I received another letter which affected me very differently. Here it is: —

'May I, at the risk of being thought very old-fashioned and narrow, protest against your admitting into your most delightful magazine sneers at the Founder of the Christian religion such as Mr. D. H. Lawrence's remark on p. 136?[1] I don't think you

---

[1] The passage from Mr. Lawrence's essay on 'Education and Sex' (which is a chapter in his *Fantasia of the Unconscious*) which distressed my correspondent was the following: —

Man remains man, however he may put on wistfulness and tenderness like petticoats, and sensibilities like pearl ornaments. Your sensitive little big-eyed boy, so much more gentle and loving than his harder sister, is male for all that, believe me. Perhaps evilly male, so mothers may learn to their cost: and wives still more.

Of course, there should be a great balance between the sexes. Man, in the daytime, must follow his own soul's greatest impulse, and give himself to life-work and risk himself to death. It is not woman who claims the highest in man. It is a man's own religious soul that drives him on beyond woman, to his supreme activity. For his highest, man is responsible to God alone. He may not pause to remember that he has a life to lose, or a wife and children to leave. He must carry forward the banner of life, though seven worlds perish, with all the wives and mothers and children in them. Hence Jesus,

can really want to drive out from the circle of your
readers the thousands of people who are alienated by
this sort of thing. I suppose that every one of us has
at some time or another rebelled against or even
blasphemed God, but the average Christian is not
much perturbed by that. It is like men throwing
stones at a star. But if the star comes down to earth
– if, as we Christians believe, God delivered himself
into our hands, then it does send cold shivers down
the spine to find such an attitude among those from
whom we were hoping to receive a new gleam of light
upon our difficult path. . . . Criticize Christians as
much as you like, and also – but in a more reverent
spirit – the Christian religion, but don't let your con-
tributors spit in the face of Jesus Christ.'

'Woman, what have I to do with thee?' Every man that lives has to
say it again to his wife or mother, once he has any work or mission
in hand that comes from his soul.

But again, no man is a blooming marvel for twenty-four hours a
day. Jesus or Napoleon or any other of them ought to have been man
enough to be able to come home at tea-time and put his slippers on
and sit under the spell of his wife. For there you are, the woman has
her world, her positivity: the world of love, of emotion, of sympathy.
And it behoves every man in his hour to take off his shoes and relax
and give himself up to his woman and her world. Not to give up his
purpose. But to give up himself for a time to her who is his mate.
– And so it is one detests the clockwork Kant, and the petit-bour-
geois Napoleon divorcing his Josephine for a Hapsburg – or even
Jesus, with his 'Woman, what have I to do with thee?' – He might
have added, 'just now.' – They were all failures.

That letter moves me; there is a simple sincerity about it that is exquisite. To alienate such a reader would be for me a personal disaster. I can do no less than try to explain.

It seems to me that the essence of the truly religious attitude is to be serious about life. (Let me say, once for all, that to be serious is not to be solemn.) The man who seeks, with the whole force of his being, a way of life which shall be in harmony with his own deepest experience, is the religious man. It does not matter whether he finds a way of life that is in accord with any known religion. There are two things, and two things alone, which distinguish the truly religious man — the passionate search for a way of life, or the truth, as some may prefer to call it ; and the loyalty to his own experience by which that search is governed. The religious man — and perhaps this distinction has become obscured in these Laodicean days — takes nothing on trust; he abides by his own experience, and by his own instinctive knowledge of what is truest and most profound in that experience. The religious man lives, or tries to live, not by faith, but by knowledge. But what he knows he does not learn by his intellect alone. If you desire to call his knowledge faith, you may; but it is better not to. It is much better to face the fact that the highest, the truest, the most permanent kind of knowledge is not rational — neither is it irrational — it is just knowledge.

Faith, as I understand the word, is a different thing altogether. Faith is the attitude of mind of the man who can accept such knowledge only when it is formulated. But the essence of this knowledge is that it is not formulable; it can be conveyed, it can be presented, but it cannot be formulated. The dogma of the Trinity, for example, is an attempted formulation of man's knowledge of God. I do not believe that anyone who has known God has ever really needed it. Whether it has ever helped anyone to know God, I cannot say. The attitude of mind of the man who can believe in God only through believing in the Trinity is what I call faith. For me, personally, faith (as I have tried to define it) is of little account. I believe that it has fettered humanity; it has hampered the advance of true knowledge and sanctified all manner of evil and cruel things. It can easily become a blasphemy against the human spirit which can only truly live by loyalty to its own experience.

Nothing, it seems to me, can be more irreligious than faith. It was faith that moved Mr. G. K. Chesterton to make the most profoundly irreligious criticism that has been made in my time: when he wrote of Thomas Hardy's work that it reminded him of 'the village atheist brooding over the village idiot.' It is one of those things that cannot be forgiven. We do not, thank heaven, get much of it in England; but in France and those countries where Catholic

58

polemists flourish, where it is a mark of intellectual
high spirits to go to Mass on Sunday and behave like
a Yahoo for the rest of the week, remarks of this
kind are frequently thought witty. If such a thing
were to creep into this magazine, it would be better
to close it down the day after.

For Thomas Hardy and Anton Tchehov are the
two truly religious writers of our time. Both of them
are called pessimistic, simply because the kind of
people who can conceive religion only in terms of
dogmatic formulæ can see in a great writer's work
only the mechanism of revelation: they are blind to
the thing revealed. But the man who can read Hardy
without being exalted by the courage and steadfast-
ness of his vision, or Tchehov without being thrilled
by the beauty of all earthly things which his delicate
fingers discover, has very little of true religion in him,
though he may be crammed to the bursting-point
with faith. Like turns to like; and the man who has
come to hate the lie in his own soul and to make what
war on it he can, is bound to respond to the work of
men like Hardy and Tchehov, who have killed the
lie in themselves, if indeed it ever existed in them.
There is no falseness in their souls or in their writings, but only purity. Even though they may never
have known it, they themselves are an answer to the
question which troubled them. In the very manner of
their asking: Does God exist? God is manifest.

I use the word God and tremble. I cannot for ever
be defining what I mean. I am not a Christian, I am
not anything, but I have been forced to the conclusion that I am religious. I would gladly leave it at
that. But (let us assume it is simply because I am
religious) I am frightened of being misunderstood.
To step an inch beyond my own knowledge is intolerable to me. I don't mind in the least when clever
people say I have been converted, or as one did the
other day, that I was running a Salvation Army and
that he knew all about it; he had seen that kind of
thing happen before. If he really did know all about
it, I think he would write rather differently – for he
is a writer. He would probably find it a little harder
to say the irresponsible things he does say, so charming and so untrue; he would be a little more certain
than he actually is about the difference between a big
writer and a little one; he would know, in short, a
little more about his own job, for he is a literary
critic. It does not matter in the least that he should
be content to dismiss me as the founder of a new
Salvation Army – it does not matter, that is, so far
as I am concerned. But I think it matters a good
deal to him; for it is a minor test of his own discrimination. I hope he is satisfied with the result; I am.

I am not afraid of using the word God because of
him or those he represents; but I am nervous of mis-
representing myself to those to whom the word is

part of a scheme. What I mean by God is not the God of those who have what I mean by faith. When I say that God is manifest in the tone and manner in which a Hardy or a Tchehov asks 'Does God exist?' I mean that the very impulse which drives such men to that utter honesty we feel in their work, is mysterious. Why is it that they *cannot* tell lies? Why is it that they *must* be loyal to their experience, and therefore to humanity? Why is it that their metal is so fine and sensitive that they instinctively obey the monition of John Donne:

> Let falsehood like a discord anger you?

And the only answer I can give that satisfies me is that they acknowledge, somehow, an allegiance to a hidden universe, therefore they command our own allegiance; they are governed by a reality which is beyond reality, therefore we are governed by them.

There is more, much more, to be said about this matter; but there is no room to say it. I must return to the question of Mr. Lawrence's article, with the hope that what I have said may be enough to make clear what I am going to say now. Whether the statement that Christ was 'a failure' is a sneer at Christianity or not depends wholly on how it is said, in the last resort upon who says it. If it is said by a man who is engaged, with all the force of his being, in the search for a way of life, it becomes not merely not a sneer but a word of import, to be underſtood. Mr. Lawrence is such a man. It is, to my mind, impossible to read either of the essays we have published, without realizing this. Their validity, the quality of being which produced them, is writ large in their subſtance. They are alive, not with the spurious vitality of modern journalism, but with an enduring spirit; it is the voice of a real person we hear in them. Mr. Lawrence is seeking a way of life; he began the search when he began to write: he has never paused.

And precisely because of that what he writes muſt be read not with the mind of faith but with the spirit of religion. In spite of (more truly, because of) its gaiety it is extremely serious. He says, in faĉt, that Chriſt, in so far as he offered humanity a way of life, was a failure. Where is the sneer in this; where the irreverence? May it not be even true? I myself believe that Chriſt's failure is his triumph: that in his life, he did once for all prove that in this world of men complete goodness and utter innocence muſt of necessity come to disaster. The life and death of Chriſt are for me the visible demonstration of the incommensurability of the ideal and the real: they repel one another, they kill one another. In his life and death we see that this opposition muſt be so; it cannot be otherwise. This necessity is a myſtery, and moſt evidently a myſtery in this, that it does not depress, but exalts the mind of the man who contemplates it. He understands at that moment that the thing we call life is but a part, and the thing we call death is also but a part. Neither is complete, neither can be comprehended in itself; they are but partial manifestations of one hidden, living and eternal reality, and those spirits for whom death is a necessity, a necessity faced and inly understood, do verily and indeed rise from the dead, for in this life they are beyond life. And some pass beyond it, as Christ passed, and some see beyond it, as Shakespeare saw: and they haunt men's minds for ever, because they have achieved a truth and revealed a mystery.

But it will be said that Mr. Lawrence, when he said that Christ was a 'failure,' meant his word in a sense less transcendental and obscure than this. I believe he did. When he says that Christ, in so far as he offered humanity a way of life, was a failure, the 'way of life' he means a way of this life that is opposed to and ended by death, not a way of the life which includes both life and death. And, unless men are prepared to take this life in their two hands and cast it from them like a muddy and clinging garment, which they are not and never will be prepared to do, then Mr. Lawrence has a right to judge the way of life which Christ offered in terms of the life to which it is professedly applied by the Christian Church. In this, as in much else, I find him infinitely more honest than his critics. For what — to take one single instance — had Christ to tell us to that tremendous problem, the relation between a man and a woman? Is it the less real to us because Christ did not face it, any more than Dostoevsky's re-creation of Christ in *The Idiot* could face it? I myself believe (though possibly Mr. Lawrence does not) that Christ was the greatest human being of whom record remains to us; and that of all men whom we know he had most of the divine in him, as I have tried to describe this mysterious element. But to say that he supplied an answer to all the questions we in our living lives have to solve is to say the thing which is not.

But, just because he did supply the answer to many questions, and revealed many mysteries, anyone who takes life seriously is bound to take him seriously also. He returns again and again to command our hearts. And to take him seriously, for some men, means to decide as honestly as they can between that part of his message which is of eternal validity and that part which is mortal as he was.

In saying that I have perhaps again offended. I cannot help it. I do not think it is possible for those who believe that Christ was a man of like passions with themselves to avoid offending those who believe he was wholly divine. But I do not believe that those to whom 'My God, my God, why hast Thou forsaken me?' is the most poignant cry in history, a con-

fession of final failure wrung from the lips of the
rarest spirit that ever inhabited a human body – are
less reverent to true religion than those to whom such
words are blasphemy. There is more than one way
of making Christ real to oneself; and I think that Mr.
Lawrence's is a necessary way at this point of time.

When, therefore, Mr. Lawrence insists that Christ
was a failure and that his words tell us nothing on a
question of such vital conern to us as the relation
between a man and a woman, he is doing no less than
his plain duty. He is not sneering at Christ; he is
regarding Christ as a present reality; it is faith that
he offends, not religion. I shall be accused of paradox
if I say that his two essays are among the most profoundly religious contributions that have been made
to this magazine; but since I believe it, I will say it.
Moreover, I will say this: I believe that faith must be
offended if we are to have any real religion in this
generation. Nevertheless, although I believe all these
things, I am sorry that anything in this magazine
should have given pain to one who has both religion
and faith. I am sorry, too, that I cannot promise it
shall never happen again. I also have my religion
and my loyalty; it includes a conviction of Mr. Lawrence's sincerity and significance. It must be left to
the future to decide whether I shall live for ever
wholly in a world of my own.

(*July*, 1923.)

Mr. Joiner's Vision

MR. JOINER SAT ON AN UPTURNED pail in his garden waiting for his supper, frowning at a hollyhock. The weather was terrible, stifling without sunshine. The silly little flower-pots stuck upside down on the tops of the flower-stakes annoyed him. They didn't even sit square; they hung jauntily, drunkenly sideways; they positively jeered at him. And he thought of their insides, a sultry mass of shiny earwigs, creatures that didn't have to breathe, didn't have, he supposed, to do anything except make nuisances of themselves. . . . There was a soft whirring in the air behind his head, as of a delicate, invisible fairy aeroplane. He turned slowly round to distinguish it. The whirring ceased. A delicate, invisible, red-hot fairy needle was pressed into the back of his neck. What the . . .!

He scratched furiously at his reddened neck, and scornfully pursued his ruminations. Why was it he had nothing to put up against such a mood and such a day?

> 'God's in His heaven,
> All's right with the world,'

sang a remembered voice from his school poetry-book. Oh, crumbs! He would just like to go and sting that chap. Robert Browning – he was dead:

lucky for him! Mr. Joiner smiled, as he did in his
moments of vision. He saw himself delicately whirring about London, ſtinging his bugbears. He
would begin with old Wotherspoon over the fence.
Wotherspoon praĉtised golf-shots with a parachute-
ball on Sunday afternoon. Because he had heard
Mr. and Mrs. Joiner laughing from the invisible
depths of their sitting-room, he had built an elaborate barricade of canvas and trellis-work to screen
himself: he had also spoiled their view. Silly old
buffaloon! It pleased Mr. Joiner to imagine himself
winging his way musically towards Wotherspoon.
He paused in his flight to consider where beſt to
ſtrike him. There was only one place, really. Eclipse
was firſt, the reſt nowhere. And that rotund expanse
of grey check trousering! Mr. Joiner almost groaned
with the pain of fruſtration.

He rose from his bucket, a happier man, and wandered indoors. 'It's no use coming in juſt yet,'
called Rosie. 'Supper won't be ready for twenty
minutes.'

'Very well, my dear.' He was engaged in ſtinging
the Archbishop of Canterbury. Did Bishops have
backs to their aprons? he wondered.

He picked up *The Adelphi*. When Bates at the
office had told him there was an article about him in
the firſt number he had laughed. 'Another chap of
the same name,' he said. 'Big family – the Joiners.

Come down in the world. Large estates at Turnham
Green: feudal – Doomsday book and that sort of
thing.'

'Is that so?' Bates had said, obviously impressed.
He was not good at seeing jokes. 'But you don't
read Shakespeare or the Bible, do you?' Bates asked.

'Good Lord, no!'

'Your wife isn't by any chance called Rosie?'

'Rosie!' Joiner had the presence of mind to laugh,
though he didn't in the least feel like laughing.
'Rosie! Why her name's Berengaria.'

'*What?*'

'Berengaria. Keep it to yourself, old man. *We*
couldn't help it.'

On his way home Joiner bought a copy. It rather
worried him in the train. He had the unusual and
uncomfortable sensation of not really existing. Every
time his eyes returned to the sentence – and it certainly fascinated him – 'He is invented. His name
is Mr. Joiner,' he felt slightly sick, as though he
were being swung through interstellar space.

And the odd thing was that as he read about himself
he seemed to remember it all; yet until he read it he
could have sworn that nothing of the kind had ever
happened to him. Yet that bit about the Prodigal
Son – he *knew* that somehow, and that about 'Make
death proud to take us' – he *knew* that too; yet he
could have sworn he hadn't known the words.

68

Surely he would have remembered if he had ever said those lines on the way to the boss's room. Why, you could hardly forget stuff like that! And now, somehow, he did remember it; remembered it better than anything else. It seemed to be stored away in some part of him where things never had been stored before — in the pit of his stomach, for instance, in the base of his spine, in some cell, perhaps, that was the centre of him when he was born, the first element of himself that harboured in his mother's womb, an element round which the rest of him had grown till it was hidden and overlaid.

And for some instinctive reason he tore out 'Mr. Joiner and the Bible' before he showed *The Adelphi* to Rosie. 'Ads!' he explained. 'Can't stand ads mixed up with the reading.' He tucked the torn-out pages away in his cash-box, together with his Savings Bank book. They were precious to him; but he thought of them with a kind of fear.

That night, at supper, he said nonchalantly:

'I say, Rosie, you don't remember my borrowing your Bible, do you?'

Rosie dropped her knife and stared at him.

'No-o,' she said. 'But —'

'But what?'

'I found the Bible downstairs in your chair, one morning. And, the night before —'

'Well?'

69

'You said something, when you came to bed, about the Prodigal Son. I can't remember what it was; but it was lovely – and so were you,' she added quickly.

'Lovely!' gasped Mr. Joiner. 'Good Lord!'

'No, that's not what I mean. You weren't any different to look at, but – I wish we could be always like that. I feel – oh, I don't know – that's what we were meant to be. Everybody,' she added vaguely.

There were tears in Rosie's eyes. Mr. Joiner jumped up and kissed her. She would not let him go; she held her head buried in his Harris-tweed; then she pulled his head down to the level of her lips.

'I think – I don't know –' she whispered, 'I'm going to have a baby.'

'Good Lord!' said Mr. Joiner.

After that life began to be rather mysterious for him. He was happy in all sorts of ways: happy at the thought of a child, for their first and only one had died at birth, and all but killed Rosie, too; happy at this queer feeling he had whenever he looked at his wife, as though he were seeing her for the very first time. But these things were only part of another feeling, vague, deep, and disturbing, which returned at unexpected moments, and for which happiness was not the name at all. He was being taken in charge by something, being driven not unkindly, being made to fulfil things. There was even a note in his voice which he couldn't recognize as being

wholly his own. Not that it belonged to anyone else.
It was his, all right, in some way or other. But he
couldn't produce it; it produced itself, and he never
knew quite when it was coming. He found himself
saying odd, rather nice things to people in trams,
and when people heard them they smiled as though
his voice were a kind of restful music. He was quite
certain it wasn't what he said – they smiled quite
differently at his best jokes – it was the voice.
Besides, he had peculiar fancies. He fancied that
this child of his was going to be amazingly beautiful.
He began to look at himself very hard in the glass
while he was shaving, and there were moments when
he thought he saw, as it were, at the back of his
reflection in the mirror, the outlines of a face, the
depths of eyes, a secret line of lips that were not his
own – and yet they were. And the depths of those
eyes, when he looked into them, were so profound,
so still and so serene, that he felt that the child whose
they were to be must be a genius. Mr. Joiner had
no better word for what he meant; but he did not
mean that exactly.

All these things thrilled and disturbed him. Moments came when he felt that something quite preposterous might be required of him. That was all
right. What was not all right was the sense that if
the something preposterous *were* required of him he
would do it without a murmur, with a kind of deep

71

and secret acquiescence. It was all quite indefinable; he could not have spoken of it: but sometimes, when he was looking at Rosie as if for the very first time, their eyes met, and he felt that she knew what was going on, and because she knew she also knew it was best to say nothing. Moreover, besides this state of fear and exaltation, Mr. Joiner had his moments of depression, when without warning he seemed to fall clean through the floor of this heaven where he understood and obeyed. He had one such moment when he was sitting on the upturned pail; but, as we have seen, he had his own methods of escaping them.

Mr. Joiner put the book down and stared at the inverted flower-pots. They looked to him like funny little invisible men each with his hat at a different angle. 'Nineteen jolly good boys – all in a row,' he murmured. It was the first comic song he had ever heard. He wondered how big he was when he first heard it. So small that it had sounded like thunder in his ears, terrifying and not comic at all. What a dark and unknown place the world had been, how strange and incalculable! Then another of his odd fancies took hold of him. It struck him that the world ought not to have been strange. There had been a mistake: somehow men had made a mess of things; above all, of themselves. Things were so bad because they themselves were blind: they had lost touch; they could not respond; they were fragmentary instead of whole. And, if they held the thread for a minute, they lost it again, and began to wander about in the darkness, leaning on laws and dogmas and policemen and armies, on anything except themselves. And so, working in the darkness, with mere fragments of their powers, they had built for themselves a monstrous habitation in the image of their stunted souls.

Because they had lost the thread. Even Tolstoi had lost the thread. How could little men help themselves?

A new generation, murmured Mr. Joiner. A generation that should not be divided from its heritage or from itself. Men and women who should never have forgotten the freedom, the pride, the unity of their own being; who knew compulsion when it came, and whence it came; who could do no other than obey themselves; men and women who were whole.

And even while he thought these thoughts, and while he looked with love and fear into the eyes of the child of his soul, who had risen before him to embody them, Mr. Joiner felt sad, for he could plainly read in those eyes that there still would be many mistakes, many sufferings, many disappointments; yes, and many treacheries, many stonings and many denials before these things should be.

(*July*, 1923.)

73

On Editing; and on Romanticism

OF LATE I HAVE RECEIVED MANY letters, which arouse in me pride and fear: a momentary pride that anything I have said or done should have found a response in such natures, an incessant fear leſt I should at any time and in any way betray the truſt that has been placed in me. And it seems to me that this fear is the moſt precious thing that has come to me as a writer. The pride laſts but an inſtant, and vanishes; the fear remains. It has become as it were a companion and a familiar, so that I have been able to look into its face and gaze into its eyes.

Those eyes are deep. I feel that, were I only to look long enough into them, I should see ſtrange things. But this I dare not. I hold to the firſt simple direct glance into them. That has meaning enough to suffice me, meaning enough to overwhelm me almoſt.

This, then, is what I see. The fear of failing those others is a present warning not to fail myself. It will not help me not to fail those others if I think of them, if I begin to consider what may hurt and offend them, and to soften this and exclude that because it may cause them pain and alarm. On the contrary, if I once begin to do that I shall have begun to fail them; I shall have begun to write and to publish less than the truth as I feel it.

That, it seems to me, is the obligation I have undertaken: to write and to publish what I feel to be true. Not what I *think* is true: I can make mistakes about that, without any consciousness of wrong. And where a mistake is a matter of indifference, at worst no more than a prick to an intellectual vanity, there the assertion is not worth making. What one feels to be true is quite another affair. Now the whole man is involved. If he is mistaken in his feeling for truth, the very roots of his being are troubled and torn. When through his whole being there comes a flash of sudden awareness of unity within him, and from some place that he scarcely knew leaps up a sense of knowledge and a sense of oneness in that which knows; when his deepest, unfamiliar self rises and takes possession of all that he is, body and mind and soul, and declares: *This is true*, – then, if he is wrong, it is disaster and dismay.

Yet perhaps the man to whom that truly happens never can be mistaken. If his deepest, unfamiliar self has risen and taken possession and pronounced:*This is true*, perhaps indeed it *is* true, for ever and ever. For this mysterious judgment is pronounced first and foremost upon a man's own acts. Of a man's acts many are indifferent – even this also may be a mark of imperfection: were we more truly living, perhaps our smallest acts, having the self in its oneness directly behind them, would be no longer indifferent but vital – but as we are, many, nay most of our acts are indifferent. But a moment comes when the whole being is awakened and on the alert: a crucial act is coming to birth. And on this judgment is pronounced. *This is right*, or *That is wrong*; and from that judgment there is no appeal.

Writing is an act. It may be an indifferent act, as the modern newspaper too plainly shows. Or it may be a crucial act. But it is the writer's own act. He can know, beyond all appeal, whether it is true. Whether his truth can be communicated, whether others can be made to feel it as he felt it – is beyond his knowledge and control. Some men are born with this compulsive gift; to others it is denied. Nevertheless, it seems impossible that a writer whose words were endorsed by his deepest self should utterly fail of hearers. But, at all events, a writer knows whether what he writes is engaging in some strange way all he knows and feels and is.

So much for the writer. But the editor is in a different case. There is the writing of others about which he feels in something of the same way as a man feels about his crucial acts. He reads a story, an essay, and with his whole being he pronounces 'This is true; this is living.' Then, and then only, he knows beyond all doubt that it is not a trick, that this piece of writing engaged the deepest self of the author.

He, in his wholeness, responds to the utterance of the author, in his wholeness.

Now, by the very nature of things, that cannot always be happening. An editor, even if his sensibility were as perfect as his sincerity, could not always *know* in this clear and incontrovertible way that all he published was true. The amount of writing coming to him which can be known for true in this way is never enough to fill his pages. What shall he do then? In ideal conditions, where printers did not work in sixteens, and nobody minded if a magazine was twenty pages one month and two hundred the next, no doubt he would stop where he was absolutely certain. But that is impossible. So he begins to choose writing because of its interest, which is a different quality from felt truth. If a piece of writing is interesting and he has no sense of falsity or trickery in it; if it feels to him honest, which again is a different thing from feeling true, he lets it in. He has done his best: the material of which he could be *certain* has failed him. He is moving now in the shadowy world of opinion. The difference is that whereas before he would have risked everything on his conviction of truth ('If this is not true, then there is no truth in me; if this is no good, then I am no good' is his feeling), now he cannot risk everything on his own conviction, simply because the conviction has never existed.

These then are the limits of possibility within which an editor's tacit obligation to be true to himself can be kept. But one thing is certain. If the offence or the pain is to be given, it will be given only by those writings of whose truth he is convinced. With the other kind — the interesting and the honest — he does not take risks: he takes risks only when he is certain, for only then *must* they be taken (after all, he does not take risks for fun), and then also he is hardly aware of having taken them.

A clever young man called Mr. Mortimer — perhaps he is not young: but he seems to be — who writes in the *New Statesman*, lately asserted that a great victory of classicism has overtaken modern English literature. He was very pleased about it, and it struck me that he must have an unusual capacity for delighting himself, seeing that the only evidence of victory he produced was the award of the Hawthornden Prize to Mr. David Garnett's *Lady into Fox*, which is about as classical as a carved cocoanut, with much the same high polish and the same intrinsic importance. But 'twas a famous victory.

In the course of his magnification of a stuffed swallow into a summer, however, Mr. Mortimer let drop a remark for which I am grateful. The opposition to this victorious tide of classicism, it appeared, is centred in this magazine: the Romantics were making 'a last despairing stand' in *The Adelphi*. I am not conscious of any feeling of desperation, nor have I found any of my colleagues down in the mouth. If classicism is to go on winning such victories so many miles away from the real field of battle, the struggle will be over without its having fired a shot of the slightest consequence. It might as well advance into action with a pop-gun.

Not but what I am inclined to believe that the elements of a real struggle might be found. But I do not think the opposed forces are Romantic and Classic. If they are, I should advise the enemy to choose a more advantageous terrain than *Lady into Fox*. And in any case, I do not see that it is my business to commence hostilities. For me, it would be a great waste of time. I do not see anything worth fighting in the field of literature: what I dislike — and there are many things I dislike — does not seem to me worth powder and shot. If battle there is to be, it will come without my choosing. A giant will arise whom I shall have to slay, lest he slay me. Then I shall slay, or be slain. But I do not see him yet. Until I do, sufficient for the day. . . . I can see no good whatever in a premature and artificial defining of the issues. They will emerge naturally, if they emerge at all.

That is to say, I am always ready to define my own position to the best of my ability. So far as I myself see clearly, there will I advance and plant this yellow flag. But I am not going to define my position in relation to the position of an enemy I do not recognize as a real one. At the moment I can see nothing in front of me to make me pause. What is toward on the far left and the distant right —

Who loses and who wins; who's in, who's out —

is no concern of mine.

But Mr. Mortimer's description of *The Adelphi* as the last stronghold of romanticism I cheerfully accept. *Foveo Danaos et dona ferentes*. (Which, being interpreted, is: 'I smile welcome to the "classicists" even when they hand me a brick.') Not that I believe for a moment that it is a true description. If I did I should not have doctored my quotation. As it is I gladly take the Wooden Horse within my walls: I will even give it a feed of cardboard oats, by saying that, on the whole, I think it is very true that I myself am a Romantic. But since nobody ever knows what anybody else means by that word, I shall do my best to make clear what it means for me. I suppose that, if I were a tactician, I should just accept the label at the face-value Mr. Mortimer so rashly gives it, and say that, since a Romantic is a person who sees no real importance in *Lady into Fox*, I am indeed a Romantic, oh, very much so. But the main point of *The Adelphi* is that it is not a place for the display of literary, or religious, or ethical, or any other tactics. It was begun not least because we were tired of those things, and because we believed that some other people were tired of them also: wherein we were more correct than men are wont to be in such surmises.

No tactics, therefore; but strategy. And the best strategy, seeing that there is no enemy of consequence visible, seems to me that I should seize the opportunity of consolidating my own position; that I should accept the designation Romantic and try to give it a content of more importance than one based on an opposition, which I do not greatly feel, to a book that does not greatly interest me. One might as well define a Romantic as one who prefers green 'bus-tickets to red ones, as I do.

Now, in the first place, there is no point, in English conditions, in opposing Romanticism to Classicism. In England there never has been any classicism worth talking about: we have had classics, but no classicism. And all our classics are romantic. That is to say, the *decorum* the great English writers naturally observe is one that they fetch out of the depths in themselves. It is not imposed by tradition or authority. There is a tradition in English life and English literature, of course, but it is not on the surface; it is not formulated or formulable, any more than the tradition of English politics is formulated or formulable. It is something you have to sense by intuition, if you are to know it at all. The English writer, the English divine, the English statesman, inherit no rules from their forbears: they inherit only this: a sense that in the last resort they must depend upon the inner voice. If they dig deep enough in their pursuit of self-knowledge – a piece of mining done not with the intellect alone, but with the whole man – they will come upon a self that is universal: in religious terms, the English tradition is that the man who truly interrogates himself will ultimately hear the voice of God, in terms of literary criticism, that the writer achieves impersonality through personality.

That, in relation to the Latin and Continental tradition, is an attitude which may be fairly described as Romantic; but to bring this time-honoured opposition across the Channel is absurd. Romanticism, as I have tried to describe it, is itself the English tradition: it is national, and it is the secret source of our own peculiar vitality. In England it is the classicist who is the interloper and the alien. And he has always been an insignificant person over here. Sometimes he has been *à la mode:* he was so for some time in the eighteenth century, and I am perfectly prepared to believe he is in the swim again at this very moment. But that is no more important than an exotic fashion in trousers. He *cannot* establish himself here; he may be a pastime for the *dilettanti;* his elegance may be attractive, but it is always the slightly excessive elegance of the outsider. And that is why the opposition between classicism and romanticism, which has been profound enough in Latin countries, has never been a thing of any significance among ourselves.

In other words – and these incessant changes of angle have a value as showing the interdependence of literature and religion – Great Britain is a Protestant country. I do not mean that it might not perfectly well have remained Catholic, provided that a special national dispensation had been arranged for it. But its Catholicism would never have been, and never will be, the real thing. Romantic Catholicism, after all, is a contradiction in terms. Catholicism stands for the principle of unquestioned spiritual authority outside the individual; that is also the principle of classicism in literature. The English nature is instinctively rebellious to such a principle. It is willing to accept its temporal ruler as its spiritual head, simply in order to politicize, to make amenable to coercion and control, the vehicle of spiritual authority. To some minds this will always appear scandalous and sacrilegious in the extreme; to others – and these see more clearly – it is the most practical form a negation of external spiritual authority can take.

It is, indeed, a commonplace that individualism – which is only another aspect of Romanticism – is in our British bones. The trouble with us, at the present time, is that we do not carry our Individualism far enough; we are not Romantic enough, nor Romantic in the right way. For there are not, as some people seem to think, a thousand and one ways of being Romantic. It is not at all the same thing as libertarianism or egalitarianism; it is essentially a search for reality through the self, and an acceptance of what one discovers there. And what one does discover there, if one looks hard enough, is something beyond all personality – call it the voice of God, call it the individual in his wholeness, call it a sense of loyalty to the hidden principle of life itself. Romanticism is the discovery and discrimination of inward reality; that is the end by reference to which alone Romanticism can be truly defined, in the light of which alone it has validity and value.

, Therefore, it is not libertarian or egalitarian. Ultimately it demands a complete surrender to something that is not in the least like my vain, puny, querulous *ego*; and not only does it demand this surrender of myself to my self, but it demands that I should surrender to achieved completeness in others. There are not many of them, but when we meet them, in person or in their work, we have to surrender, knowing that what we do is good. Some are leaders and some are led; some discover truth, others recognize the truth when it is declared to them. It has happened again and again in the history of mankind. But Romantic leadership is freely chosen and freely acknowledged; the principle of classical leadership is that obeisance is made to the office or to the tradition, never to the man.

I might go on, but my space is ending. Perhaps I have said enough at the moment to distinguish clearly between the two great principles of Classicism and Romanticism, in literature and religion and morality. For they are indeed great principles, and not lightly to be evoked by young men who know so little about their own professed cause as to make a drawing-room *bibelot* representative of it. When a classicist comes along who knows as much about his own creed as I know about mine – then we may prepare for battle. But that is not the sort of opposition we have to fear in this country. On the other side are ranged not classicists but false and incomplete Romantics, people who for the sake of a little prestige in a little coterie try to wear their rue with a difference imported from Paris. And, of course, it is only by a figure of speech that I say they are ranged on the other side; they are skirmishing on the far horizon, sounding alarums on penny trumpets, and beating excursions on twopenny drums, capturing Hawthornden prizes and appointing one another field-marshals.

(*August*, 1923.)

Is The Play the Thing?

I LATELY CONFESSED THAT I scarcely ever go to the play, and I gave some account of an unwonted venture, which cost me eight and sixpence. I have not, indeed, been to the play since then; but I have done something which is to me much more remarkable: I have read a whole volume of 400 large pages, of which half is in praise of the modern English drama and the other half in criticism — a mild word, that — of the Elizabethan drama. I have read it; I have been absorbed by it; I have been almost convinced. The book — let me say quite plainly that it is a most excellent book, written by a master of his subject, and producing on the reader that rare and delightful sense of comfort that only mastery can produce: that it is a book that every one who cares for literature should get hold of somehow — is William Archer's *The Old Drama and the New*.

It was given me by a good friend. Nevertheless, I don't suppose that, even out of friendship, I should have read it, had it not happened on one lazy August evening I took down my copy of the plays of John Ford. It is a good many years since I read Ford. I used to have a copy of *The Broken Heart* which looked so like a small Bible that I could read it in the school chapel, and I did. A little later I bought for myself a copy of Ford and Massinger in a single volume, and I read that. Somehow, I cannot imagine how, I persuaded myself in my youth that John Ford was a considerable person. Perhaps it was intellectual snobbery: the Elizabethans had a tremendous prestige when I reached years of discretion. I hope also that I was moved by the one or two passages of charming poetry – skin-deep, it is true, but of an attractive complexion – which are in his plays. Whatever the cause, John Ford certainly became a figure to me: he was somebody, and he was an Elizabethan. And I had a vague conception of a subtle, fantastic, melancholy nature, expressing itself in a language of which I dimly remembered the quality as an ineffectual purity. He was, I thought, the man for me, on that warm August evening. So I took him down.

It was a shock. If John Ford is not nothing, he is next door to it. Of late years, I must explain, almost every Elizabethan except Shakespeare has begun to disappoint me. Shakespeare grows steadily bigger and bigger in my mind, and the rest grow smaller and smaller. Even Webster strikes me as being very little if not a poet, and as being a smallish kind of poet beside Donne. The line—

'Cover her face: mine eyes dazzle: she died young,'

which for at least ten years of my life I dutifully

87

believed to be at the very pinnacle of dramatic elo-
quence, has of late seemed to me a piece of spoof.
The effect is of the nature of an optical illusion. The
imagination is not there, neither is the poetry. There
remains the magical and uncouth Marlowe; there
remains Ben Jonson, who is something, something I
do not particularly like, but undeniably *something*,
against which one can, as it were, bang one's head
and feel the ensuing bump. (And, by the way,
nobody more than Mr. T. S. Eliot has helped me to
understand what that something is.) I am still
attracted to Middleton, and I find a rather pleasing
absence of this optical illusion of poetry in Massinger. But the Elizabethan drama as a whole has of
late seemed to me thin stuff compared to Shakespeare. It is, of course, Shakespeare himself who
knocks the bottom out of it; and when one has been
reading, as I have been reading, little else than Shakespeare for four years, it begins to be almost painfully
clear that, both as dramatist and poet, Shakespeare
was of a totally different *kind* from any of his contemporaries. He is not the bright particular star in a
constellation; he is another universe. And perhaps
one of the reasons why we know so little about him,
is that his contemporaries felt it. He must have been
mysterious and paralyzing to them.

Nevertheless, though I was accustomed to find the
minor Elizabethans 'gin to pale their ineffectual fires,

I was not prepared to see the star of John Ford drop clean out of the sky as it did for me that evening. His characters appeared to me convulsive marionettes, his versification undistinguished to the verge of vulgarity, and his notion of a dramatic situation puerile. Bianca's behaviour in *Love's Sacrifice* was clean beyond my comprehension; she is a psychological monstrosity. The incestuous love of Giovanni and Annabella in *'Tis Pity She's a Whore* appeared to me devoid of all imaginative realization, and therefore merely a gratuitously unpleasant piece of melodramatic invention, culminating in a senseless piece of savagery. I was indeed so perplexed by the nothingness of this elaborate brutality that I cast about for some explanation. Ford was not a fool; neither were his two superiors in the manipulation of the crudities of Italianate revenge-plots, Webster and Tourneur, fools. Why, then, did they do what they did? And the only answer I could find was that, wanting to write tragedies, they found that further advance along the true tragic road was barred to them by Shakespeare's achievement. So they flung themselves on to the Italianate horrors as a way of escape. They could spill more blood, present more incests, depict more anthropophagi than Shakespeare. He had merely put out Gloucester's eyes; they would – do what they did. I thought, and still think, it may have been another case of the despair

89

that fell upon John Milton when he thought of Shakespeare:

'But thou, our fancy of itself bereaving,
  Dost make us marble with too much conceiving.'

And they had not — even the most gifted of them — Milton's parts or his probity. If we can't be tragedians, they said, we will be Grand Guignol: and they were.

However this may be, on that night I was disappointed and disgusted with John Ford. Still worse, I was bored, unutterably bored by him. I would gladly have given every line he wrote for one short poem of Thomas Hardy's. And it seemed to me preposterous that such inferior stuff should be allowed to retain the prestige it has acquired. Why has nobody made an onslaught upon it? Perhaps (I thought) because nobody really reads it, except people engaged in taking degrees in English literature, and they — it is well known — have other things to think about than whether what they read is worth reading. When they have their degrees they promptly and very wisely forget all the stuff they have had to wade through; or they become professors and dare not blow the gaff on their own stock-in-trade. I sighed, thinking that there is still a great deal of work to be done by an honest and disinterested criticism; and then I took down William Archer's book. For the moment I was sick of the old drama; I wanted to taste the new. And lo and behold! there was this veteran critic valiantly engaged in doing the very thing that I demanded. He was bowling over the minor Elizabethan dramatists, as dramatists, like so many skittles. And I defy anyone to show that his destructive criticism is not substantially sound. But when I found him expressing my own heretical opinion concerning

'Cover her face: mine eyes dazzle: she died young,'

I was almost enraptured. This, I said in my joy, is the dramatic critic for me. And on the whole he is. I do not believe there is another dramatic critic in the world who could have written a book so comprehensive, so sane, so interesting, and so evidently honest as this book of William Archer's.

Not that I agree with it all. When he says, for instance, that Ford's spirit was more subtle than Webster's, I disagree entirely. Of the two Webster was the subtle one, even though he was the bloodier. And when he says, in criticism of Shakespeare, that he had no conception of the idea of progress, I do not so much disagree as I am astonished at a remark which may or may not be true, but is, in either case, without any real import. Nor am I sure that I agree with his fundamental position that since the evolution of the drama has actually been towards an art of

91

realistic representation we must necessarily accept this as its ideal end. But it is a position I can understand, and one which seems to me a perfectly adequate foundation for a substantial edifice of criticism such as Mr. Archer builds upon it. And on the negative side at least Mr. Archer's argument is absolutely convincing when he maintains

'that the people who extol the semi-barbarous drama of the minor Elizabethans as something vastly superior to the drama of to-day have no conception of the true essence of the drama, and found their opinion (in so far as it has any rational foundation at all) on a palpable confusion between drama and lyric poetry.'

In other words, Mr Archer's blade is double-edged: one edge is the assertion that most of the minor Elizabethans are not dramatic, the other the assertion that a great many modern English playwrights are.

Now the logician will say that everything depends upon the meaning of the word *dramatic*. And, of course, it does. I cannot define it, nor do I think very much of Mr. Archer's attempt to do so, for he defines it not essentially but in terms of that process of evolution towards realistic representation which he considers necessary and inevitable. But definitions are not everything: and I, as a very amateur in this matter, know that there is a profound difference between the poetic and the dramatic. What is poetic *may* also be dramatic; but it seldom is. What is dramatic *may* also be poetic; and that, too, seldom happens. By poetic I mean not metric or rhythmic, but an expression in language of the creative imagination. Some drama, in short, is creative literature; and as such will last for all time. A great deal of drama, which is perfectly good as drama, is not creative literature at all.

Mr. Archer's main positive contention is that there is a great deal of good drama now written by English playwrights. Very likely that is true. I am going to see for myself, when I get the chance. But he seems to lose sight of the further question: Is this drama truly creative literature? The drama, he maintains, is a separate art, following its own destiny. That is obviously true. But it seems also to be true that unless the drama is also creative literature, it cannot last for centuries. Sometimes, indeed, it lasts a surprisingly long while: a good primitive dramatic situation may keep a thing like *Box and Cox* flourishing through generations. But the element of true permanence seems to be outside all purely dramatic excellence. It resides in the creative truth of the representation of human life, whether that is expressed in poetry or prose. In other words, a drama, to endure, must have style. It must be the rendering in language of real vitality of an author's unique vision of human life. Its effectiveness as drama is here irrelevant; it has to be effective as literature.

How much of modern English drama will satisfy this test, I do not know: I am altogether too ignorant of the subject-matter. But it seems to me that Mr. Archer never puts this crucial question quite clearly to himself. He is concerned with the art of the drama, not with the art of literature. And many of his quotations, which like a courageous and honest man he always brings forward to support his judgments of modern plays, are convincing as drama and unconvincing as literature. Mr. Drinkwater's *Abraham Lincoln* is a clear case of good drama and bad literature. Sir Arthur Pinero, whom Mr. Archer praises with a splendid discrimination according to his own standards, is a more doubtful example, to judge by the quotations. The portion of Mr. Lennox Robinson's *The Lost Leader* which is given, in which the doctor accidentally hypnotizes the old Irishman Lucius and so evokes the revelation that the old man is Parnell, is as plainly effective drama as it is plainly inferior literature. The opening scene of Mr. Galsworthy's *The Silver Box* looks like good drama and good writing, both.

I am not complaining that Mr. Archer does not employ both standards of criticism. The obvious duty of a dramatic critic is to appraise plays as drama: but it is the obvious duty of the literary critic to appraise them as literature. This Mr. Archer is inclined to forget when he champions the authors of modern plays; but when he attacks the plays of the minor Elizabethans he himself as often as not is condemning them not for ineffectiveness as drama — a good many of them are dramatically much more effective than he admits — but for their deficiencies as literature. They are not 'just representations of human nature,' to use Dr. Johnson's phrase. But it is doubtful whether the drama as a separate art does depend on 'just representations of human nature.' The *sens du théâtre* is not a sense of universal psychology; but of a very particular and unrepresentative sort of psychology. Only when this is combined with a creative and comprehensive vision of life, so that the particular demand be satisfied without doing violence to the universal necessity, shall we find drama that is of more than ephemeral consequence.

And it does not really matter whether the dramatist's representation shows us the superficies of modern life as we see it. The important thing is that he should give us a revelation of the profound realities of life as we have felt and experienced them: that he should make vocal our dumb delights and dismays. If he can do this within the strict limits of a peculiar technique, he is a great artist. In spite of

Mr. Archer's persuasiveness, I do not suppose these are more plentiful to-day than they were in the days of Shakespeare.

Nevertheless, though I do not expect to find many *Cherry Orchards* or even many *Hedda Gablers* among the modern plays in London, I shall make trial of them, and I shall expect to enjoy myself and make some minor discoveries. I shall be very annoyed with Mr. Archer if I do not. But my first concern now remains as it was two months ago: to see the new film by Charlie Chaplin. I *know* I shall get something from that. It is called *The Pilgrim*, and it is to be 'released' — the word suggests that there must be a venomous spring in a coil of films — on the very day on which these words appear.

(*August*, 1923.)

A Moment of Peace

THERE ARE MOMENTS, I VERILY BElieve, when one loses one's soul; moments, hours, days, when that which one is, mysteriously dissolves away. I am silent, but I cannot be still; I speak, but the words are not my own. I do nothing and I am tired; I do many things, and I am also tired, but not a whit more tired than if I had done nothing. For all those many things make one nothing: not one of them has been my own. This is the fatigue of nothingness, not the rich and brooding weariness of activity.

To achieve an act that is our own is to create. Whether it is a word spoken out of our entirety, a sentence as it were endorsed by our secret being, which reveals to us a truth of which we did not know we were aware; or the word of another that we read and recognize within ourselves as valid, that finds its way to the depths and there awakes some hidden potency; or some quite simple gesture — nothing more, perhaps, than a hand on a friend's arm or a passing Good-night — which suddenly claimed the whole of us for its begetter, leaped out of the mists of our self-ignorance and took possession of its rightful throne — each one of these is an act of creation. Such acts as these bring their weariness and bring it quickly — we are none too used to them — but the weariness is rich and full.

The fatigue of nothingness is poor and empty, like the yawn of nervousness compared with the yawn of sleep. It is a protest against an absence, not a recognition of a presence: the drooping of the unwatered flower, not the bending of the laden branch. It is as though that which grows above the ground were divided from that which is below — Hamlet's disease, and we cry like Hamlet:

'How weary, stale, flat, and unprofitable,
  Seem to me all the uses of the world!

But we do not leave the world; we do not go apart and wait for something that is bigger than ourselves to take possession and drive away the fretful inhabitant. On the contrary, to be left alone with ourselves, which is the condition we truly desire, seems at this moment a calamity to be shunned like the plague. There is no self to be left alone with. Peradventure he sleepeth. Wherever he may be, whatever he may be doing, he is not within reach of any call of ours. We are like empty agitated shells, mere quivering superficies: we see with our eyes alone, speak only with our lips, and we jump at the opportunity of stopping the mouths of these clamorous and insatiable members with a sensation, an excitement. They become only the more hungry and insistent.

All this is highfalutin', no doubt; but the state of soul, or the state of no-soul, is real. And one of the ways to exorcise it – not perhaps the best – is to sit down and try to draw its likeness upon paper. Even an idealized picture is better than none. The hands, the conscious mind are occupied; in the half-quiet something of that which has been lost may creep back again, even if it is only a fatigue which is not of the nerves alone.

Something did creep back. I went to bed, alone in my little house, for which I have no particular affection, but where I am at least undisturbed by alien personalities, where I feel that, if anything goes wrong with me, I have only myself to blame, where I cannot have excitement even though I crave for it. And now, having waked up, and spent a day utterly alone, having cooked myself many elaborate meals of mushrooms – I can get an enormous pound of them for sixpence – I can hardly remember how it was that I was so agitated twenty-four hours ago, when what I have now, was remote, impossible, almost unimaginable to me. I can just remember that there was something at once sinister and futile about the ticking of my clock; it seemed to have become almost the whole of me, which was sinister, and to be say-ing: 'This way – that way – no way – this way – that way – no way,' which was futile. I swayed with it in a kind of empty irritation. Years ago, that was.

Now I am myself again: nothing, as they say, to

shout about: neither particularly happy nor particularly sad: but somehow free; free from everything
except the habit of smoking cigarettes as I write.
And that annoys me only when I think about it.
But for the rest, as far as my sensation goes, free.
Free to say what I like, free to do what I like: and for
the moment what I like to do is to say what I like
here. In ten minutes I may be sick of it: then I shall
knock off. In twenty certainly I shall, for I have left
another mess of mushrooms on the stove, and when
I get up to stir them I shall not sit down again to this
sheet of paper until I have eaten them – my supper.

Yes, free. It's a queer feeling; it doesn't come to
me too often, and when it does I wish it would stay
longer. Perhaps it will: I seem to have it for longer
nowadays than I have had it for many years, in truth,
than I have ever had it. And it occurs to me that it
is as well that at this moment I like to do precisely
what I am doing: this month I have cut the time for
this essay rather short. But I was thinking things
over this afternoon while I was weeding my path.
First, I came to the knowledge that I was free, then I
wondered what I should like to do with my freedom.
I would like to go round the world, but very slowly,
and not in one of those great ships that frightened and
made me angry when I saw one for the first time in
Southampton Water the other day. It was a great
comfort to me to think that the ocean would make no

more bones of that sham-Leviathan than sham-Leviathan did of me. Not in one of those things will I go round the world. If that is civilization, civilization can go to the devil for all I care; I will follow Mr. D. H. Lawrence into rebellion, and carry my small flag in the shadow of his sombre-splendid banner.

Well, I will go round the world, and in my own way. Why not to-morrow? Because I don't want to go to-morrow. My desire is as yet only a half-desire; I will wait until it becomes a whole and overpowering one. In the meanwhile I will wait. And just now waiting, which is so often pale and nerve-fretting, seems to me a rich and full activity. I am free; I can do what I like; and what I really want to do is to wait. Just to wait. Not for anything in particular: certainly not to begin my journey round the world. I simply let that half-desire sink to the bottom of my lagoon until it grows into a whole one, till the small oyster becomes a big one, with perhaps a pearl inside. But if I think, I can think of many things I might be waiting for. But I don't believe I am really waiting consciously *for* anything. I simply want to wait, and while I am waiting, to take care I don't do anything I don't really want to do. I am a perfect whale at getting myself involved. I have had moments of awful fear regarding *The Adelphi*; I feared I had taken on a duty, assumed a responsibility, which I should have to fulfil month after month for ever.

Now, I don't feel anything of the kind. My duty is simply to tell no lies; and for the rest to follow my deepest instinct. So that if one day I feel quite surely and simply that I must begin my journey round the world to-morrow, I shall pack my bag and go to-morrow. . . . A distinct smell of burning mushrooms!

No, not burning, but – Launcelot Gobbo had the words for it – 'They did something smack, something grow to, they had a kind of taste.' Anyhow, I have eaten them and I am glad that no one was forced to dine with me.

But, to return to this waiting. I do not know what I am waiting for. If I did, I should probably not be able to wait. It may be one of many things I can think of; it may be none of these many things. I may be waiting for someone to arrive who will take over *The Adelphi* from me; or for a friend to return; or, simply, for some decision, for a road to open in front of me. I have given up taking important decisions with my head: only disasters came of that, for the head is a good servant, but a bad master; he steers one into agitations and despairs. I know him of old. Now I am content to wait, while something else – my instinct or my destiny – decides.

It is queer how long it takes one to reach even this point. It seems that my whole life up to this moment has been spent in reaching this moment – a moment with nothing particular to say for itself, no rainbow-hues, no magical gleam, nothing in the least distinguished about it, altogether a most ordinary affair – just a sense of waiting and of being content to wait. It does seem queer that one should have come such a long way – through so many infinitely more exciting moments – to find just this, and queerer still that one should be satisfied with what one has found. Not for ever. One waits unconsciously for something, without a doubt; and if the something were never to come, it would be a bad business. But the character and quality of this waiting is that one knows that something *will* come, and that one will recognize it when it does. Not to be impatient, not to expect miracles, not to be agitated whether this or that will be – this is itself, for one man at least, a miracle; and even if it does not endure, why, then –

'It shall have been;
Nor God nor demon can undo the done,
Unsight the seen.'

Now, from this undramatic pinnacle, this little hump on the plain instead of the mountain one used to expect and even to begin climbing so feverishly, one looks back. It is surprising how far and how clearly one can see from this unimpressive eminence. How far and how clearly backward; but the forward view is quite shut out. And to one man it seems that his life behind him falls into phases. There was first the long struggle to reject the conceptions of good and evil that were imposed from without; then the slow birth of the knowledge that one's good and evil are one's own; then the still more painful birth of the knowledge that this knowledge itself is of no avail, that one cannot *know* one's good and evil; then the tortured writhing into a sense that one's good is growth and one's evil is decay; then the vision that one's growth is not simple and single, that it is not a straightforward upward motion, that there is, as it were, a pole of light and a pole of darkness, a pole of striving and a pole of surrender, a growing down into the darkness and a growing up into the light, and that these two growths are but a single growth: that on the vitality of these two movements the vitality of the being itself depends. And further, at every point of new and completer knowledge, a new despair, that one cannot do what must be done simply because one *knows* it must be done. And, after each new despair, a period of waiting, of a waiting whose depth and quality changes in each phase, until one can recognize it almost as a law that the stiller, the less dramatic, the more ordinary the waiting, the greater the chance that a new path will be shown.

It seems so very little to have learned from life, so colourless, so unexciting. I can see the objections;

but I do not feel them. This looking back, this mapping out of the wavering zig-zag track, is infinitely thrilling: more thrilling still that it has brought me here, to this moment I could never have guessed nor foreseen, to this moment which, if I had foreseen it, only a few years ago, would have appeared as a moment of emptiness to be avoided, whereas, living in it now, I know it for that desired of all desirables – a moment of peace.

(September, 1923*.)*

David and Goliath

I KNEW IT WOULD HAPPEN, OF
course; nevertheless, and also of course, I was disappointed that it did. Charlie Chaplin's *The Pilgrim*
was dismissed by *The Times* in four lines of minuscule
type as 'burlesque melodrama,' which it certainly is
not, and frowned upon by the *Observer* for being
inferior to *The Kid*, which I doubt. I did not see the
other newspapers.

Why is it, I wonder, that there is no real criticism of
the cinema? Occasionally, a dramatic critic lets himself go — and lets himself go. Two years ago a whole
host of them wallowed in *The Kid*; they told us of
strong City men, with large watch-chains and
stomachs, who wept hot tears; they began to talk
about Chaplin the great actor, just as though he had
never existed before. Not one of them, apparently, had
seen *A Dog's Life*, or *Easy Street*, or *The Immigrant*,
or *Charlie the Champion*; not one of them had any
conception, based on real knowledge, of what Chaplin could and could not do, or a notion of the way he
might develop his astounding genius. But since there
was a good deal of sentimentality in *The Kid*, besides
some moments of marvellous acting, they all declared
it was Chaplin's masterpiece. It was nothing of the
kind.

There are many possible attitudes towards the

cinema. You may regard the whole institution as nauseous, and dismiss it entirely. You may acknowledge that it exists and be superior and pontifical about it: like the gentlemen who lose no opportunity of saying what a marvellous educational influence the cinema would be, if only there were more educational films. (I have seen some – *The Marriage of a Polyp* and the *Courtship of a Flounder*, where what is going on is utterly invisible to the naked eye.) Or you may regard the whole thing as a strange new social fact, to be understood and estimated: and this, I think, is the most terrifying aspect of the cinema; from this angle it becomes, together with wireless and listening-in, one of the most monstrous portents of modern times. And there is another attitude still but that may wait.

The first – the wholly negative – attitude has nothing to do with us now. The second – the pontifical – attitude is merely silly: people will not go to see educational films, and until some one who knows something of the mere technique of the cinema takes them in hand, nobody ever will go to see them. But the cinema as a social fact is interesting and alarming. I suppose not less than a million people go to the cinema every day in England. And the stuff they sit through! Without a murmur; for all one can see, utterly apathetic. They seem to be in a condition of perpetual coma, like a python after swallowing a cow.

They will swallow any number of cows apparently, slowly and monotonously ingurgitate whatever the idiots who manufacture film by the ton choose to put before them. You have the sense, as you sit there, trying to digest the cannon-ball of your own awful boredom, that no one knows anything whatever about the process in which you have rashly involved yourself. There is a great machine for the production and consumption of film. From the million-dollar man at the top to the ninepenny front-row man at the bottom there runs one endless chain of black and abysmal ignorance. The million-dollar man would probably like to supply what the public wants: the public doesn't *want* anything: it neither likes nor dislikes what is provided at the cinema: it wants nothing except *to go to the cinema*. Beyond that, it has no reaction whatever. So the million-dollar man, having nothing whatever to guide him, takes for his standard the only one that means anything to him when he is left to his own resources – money. He spends more and more money, quite witlessly. If a dog appears for a second in the film, then it must be a million-dollar dog. No horse that is not a thoroughbred; no car that is not a Rolls-Royce. It is terrifying.

The first, the foremost, and the most awful fact about the cinema is that the cinema public will swallow anything. It is one of the most powerful pieces of apparatus for the mechanization of the human universe that has yet been invented; and, for the most part, it works entirely on its own, without guidance or control. Anyone who has imagination or sensitiveness enough to feel horror, must be horrified by it. The cinema, as a social fact, does not bear thinking about too much.

Nevertheless, within this nightmare world of mechanism, which does exist and cannot be abolished by turning one's back upon it, there are a handful of men of individuality, and one man of genius. They have imposed themselves somehow: in this desert of flickering sameness they are different, some just a little, some considerably, one absolutely. On these men, and on this one man in particular, the possibility of keeping this mechanical monster under some sort of human, living control depends. Chaplin awakes the audience out of its coma into some kind of awareness: how great the awareness is, how deep it goes, I do not know. I simply have the sense that while he is on the screen the apathetic audience becomes momentarily alive. If it laughs where there is nothing to laugh at, it does not matter; it is doing and feeling something. The gloom of mere insentience is lifted. At every point he conquers the machine: he is his own million-dollar man. He composes his scenario, he produces his own film, he is his own chief actor, and he creates

himself. The worst Chaplin film – and I cannot remember one that was really bad – is by a whole
degree better than the best of any other man. It
belongs to a different kind.

First, because in its whole genesis it is a different
thing. The making of a Chaplin film is obviously
different from the making of any other. A mind, or
an instinct, with an ultimate purpose is in control.
What he desires, that – in so far as he can do it –he
does. He is not wasting his energy in trying to out-
wit some imbecile who insists on spending a million
to achieve a result that is better achieved for sixpence. Second, because his ultimate purpose is
different. He aims at amusing an audience, no
doubt; just as, in Wordsworth's sense, the poet aims
first at giving pleasure. But the giving of this pleasure is conditioned. It is conditioned by this creation of himself – the Charlie Chaplin of the hoard-
ings and the pictures, who is so different from Mr.
Charles Chaplin, the beautiful young man who is a
millionaire in California – by means of which the
pleasure has to be given. And this creation of himself, this figure of 'Charlie,' is a thing of import and
significance. It represents an attitude of rebellion
against the mechanism of life. Chaplin, as I call him
when I want to distinguish the creator from the creature 'Charlie,' has somewhere and somehow been
under the wheels of modern civilization; and he re-

members it. 'Charlie' is the embodiment of some of his resentment and contempt: he is the under-dog, who wages his incessant and spontaneous warfare against institutions and the lie of moribund ideals. I do not believe that 'Charlie' is the *conscious* creation of Chaplin, or that the things which 'Charlie' does in a film are really predetermined. They come from a natural and spontaneous adjustment to the universe; and I imagine that Chaplin himself would have almost as great a difficulty as I have in forcing the implications of his own creation into his conscious mind.

Take, for a single instance, the most wholly surprising incident in *The Pilgrim*. Charlie, the escaped convict, becomes by the accident of circumstance the minister of a Western American town, has to take the service the moment he arrives. He knows nothing about services. He manages to get through to the sermon. Then he is inspired. He mimes the fight between David and Goliath: as an achievement of miming it is astonishing, superb. His congregation is scandalized and thunderstruck: one small boy bursts in whoops of applause. I was so carried away by the moment that I simply could not realize the implicit satire on conventional religion. I remember saying to myself with heartfelt conviction: 'I wish all sermons were like that: I should go to church more often.' But it was only afterwards that I understood

how extraordinarily real that fight between the little
man and the giant had been, how 'Charlie' had sur-
rendered himself to it, how I had been carried away
by it – as a thing in itself, not as part of a scene in a
Wild West conventicle. And that congregation,
which should have been as overcome as I was, is
simply scandalized, save for one small boy! I can
read into the episode now a whole universe of meaning, and it will bear it all. And 'Charlie' himself – is
he not perpetually the David against the Goliath?
And is not the attitude of his audience generally
about as comprehending as the attitude of the congregation of Devil's Gulch?

I say again, I do not believe that Chaplin is wholly
conscious of what he does: that would be superhuman. But there is some essential truth, some fundamental rightness, in the whole attitude towards
life which he has embodied in the creation of himself
into 'Charlie.' This essential truth it is which makes
his smallest act significant. In some way, he cannot
go wholly wrong: so long as he allows 'Charlie' to
react instinctively to his circumstances. The truth
of spontaneity is in his bones; it disciplines all his
astonishing feats of sheer technique into a single
effect; it makes his films yield more and more at a
second and a third seeing; it enables this little David
to win victory after victory over the Goliath of
mechanism – in the world, in the machine of cinema

itself, in the soul of an audience, which if dead to all else, stirs at his approach.

Chaplin is a great artist in the true sense of the word. He is not merely a great actor; he belongs to another and a higher order. Those who desire to see him (as he is reported to desire to see himself) interpreting the creations of other men, do not understand what he is or what he has done. Possibly he does not understand it himself; but somewhere certainly he *knows*. If he will only trust himself, all will be well. All that criticism can do — and if it had any sense of values it would be busy with the work — is to help him to trust himself completely.

(*September*, 1923.)

On Tolstoi and Other Things

FOR MORE THAN A FORTNIGHT I
have been under the spell of Tolstoi's *War and
Peace*. I have been wandering about, in the North of
England – strange, strong and half-terrifying country
for the soft Southerner that I am – in South Germany, where it costs 5 million marks to leave your
bag in a cloak-room – and I have come to a momentary rest in Switzerland in a familiar house with a
familiar friend. And all the way the spell of Tolstoi
has been upon me.

I stood at the window of the *Hotel der Römischer
Kaiser* in Freiburg in the Breisgau: the resting-place
of the Roman Caesars, under the shadow of one of
the tall towers of the old city, where in the mellow
past more than one Holy Roman Emperor had
stayed, and in the warm autumn evening I felt the
magic of that great tradition. It seemed that all that
was hard and stubborn and stern in the *imperium
Romanum* was softened and subdued into an element
akin to the old gold of the early October sun. I was
in a place where alien threads of European destiny
were knotted and intertwined, where old identities
had been lost in a warm golden haze; a matrix, a
womb of Europe, where things sank backward and
were changed, where the Rhine begins her north-
ward and the Rhone her southward flow. The city

seemed ripe like a medlar and sweet in its decay. On each monument stood some Holy Roman Emperor of stone, clad in rococo Roman armour with plumes sprouting out of his Roman helmet, and a ponderous Latin inscription to celebrate his virtues. And while I stood listening at the window there came to me, as there comes inevitably to anyone whose mind and senses are alert at the touch of an unfamiliar emanation from men or the earth which shapes them, the symbol of all that held me enchanted and wondering there. The Salvation Army came marching by. Oh, not the Salvation Army we know. I was aware of it first as a choir of rich, velvet voices singing a German hymn; then I heard the thrumming of many guitars, a sound intolerably sweet and sun-warmed and old – humanly old, a cadence softened by many centuries. I put my head out of the window and looked down. I don't know what I expected to see. Perhaps a band of those rococo Roman legionaries with a forest of swollen plumes in their helmets; perhaps Freiburgers in eighteenth-century knee-breeches and Breisgau girls in flowery hats of straw. But nothing of these at all. Real Salvation Army caps, and Salvation Army bonnets. It was inevitable and right; but I could never have guessed it. 'Blood and Fire' and those voices, those guitars! There was the name, there was the uniform, but the spirit how changed! Just as I know not which homely and

Imperial, holy and Roman, Conrad or Otto or Fried-
rich had smiled his amiable smile at me from under
his Roman helmet, and nodded acquaintance with
his sumptuous plumes of ſtone.

Yet in all this Tolſtoi was somehow involved. All
that I felt, all that I saw, seemed to fall into its place
in the vaſt landscape of *War and Peace*. A sense of
the inevitable in human hiſtory, of something againſt
which the puny personal and conscious will cannot
prevail, of deſtinies of earth and men that muſt be
accomplished, enfolded Freiburg in the ſtory of
Moscow. Napoleon had overrun the Breisgau also,
held it for many years. What mark had he left? No
more than he left on the plains of Russia. He had
dissolved the Holy Roman Empire; yet its queer
shadowy reality remains as sensible as the smell of
an autumn vineyard. Neither he nor Bismarck has
changed it, for it is an attitude of the human soul.
Sit ſtill in Freiburg for an hour, with your mind and
senses open to what may be wafted in, and you will
know that in spite of Napoleon who forced it together
and Bismarck who welded it in 'blood and iron,' the
German Empire may fall asunder to-morrow, like

'the ripeſt mulberry
That will not hold the handling;'

not through the machinations of the French or the
failure of the English, but simply because the in-
116

ſtinctive will to be a German Empire is not there. 'Blood and iron,' like 'Blood and fire,' is only a phrase in Southern Germany. The reality is soft and indifferent and old, sweet-smelling, rotten-ripe with centuries of *la douceur de vivre*.

But that, I suppose, is politics. Anyhow, Tolſtoi knew far more about politics than the politicians, as he knew far more about war than the generals. He knew that politics and warfare are, when the empty labels and the foolish hiſtories are discarded, a manifeſtation of the inſtinctive human soul. Knowledge of the human soul beneath all its pretences and self-delusions: by that a man is truly great, and that Tolſtoi had. In such measure that he was

> 'like a Colossus; and we petty men
> Peep under his huge legs and peer about
> To find ourselves dishonourable graves.'

What that man knew and told in *War and Peace* is so tremendous that we are left wondering at what he knew and did not tell. He did not tell all his knowledge, any more than Shakespeare told all his. Perhaps it was knowledge of a kind that cannot be told; knowledge of a kind that indeed would make Tolſtoi's dismissal of himself and of Shakespeare a simple and inevitable geſture. Shakespeare ſtopped writing, Tolſtoi ſtopped writing. I know in my bones that it was from the same cause; they knew they were engaged in an attempt to express the inexpressible; they were tired of the failure they knew to be inevitable. They went back to simple things and held their peace.

These last years I have been haunted by two mysteries: the mystery of Shakespeare and the mystery of Tolstoi. They occupy my mind whenever it is vacant; and it seems to me now that I understand them more nearly than ever before. I have always felt — and I do not believe it is altogether vain imagination — that other writers yielded up their secret when I have wrestled with them: but these two have remained. And now I begin to understand them also. They are not less mysterious. A mystery is not less a mystery for being understood; because we never do *understand* it. We know it. And this knowing of a mystery is not accomplished by the mind: it comes only with a sense of a like mystery in ourselves. It is a direct communion between mystery and mystery. My mystery may be a little one; theirs, I know, were big ones: but they are of the same kind, and they communicate.

But how to describe this mystery? I do not know: unless it could be done in terms of that process of growth which brings us to the point when we suddenly realize that certain things are important and the rest trivial. The mystery peeps out for me quite plainly when in his later years Tolstoi asks in his conversation about a writer: 'Does he believe in God?' Or when he says, having read Andreyev's work, 'That man believes in God and is terrified.' Questions and judgments which seem to some people silly. If they would only consider what manner of man he was that asked, and what he knew and had done, they might begin to suspect that the questions and the judgments contain a deeper meaning than they are yet fit to know. What God it was that Tolstoi worshipped, I cannot describe; but I think I know. It was a God that includes Christ; it was a God that, unlike Christ, was also dark and terrible; it was the God who is the God of the Matthew of Mr. Lawrence's poem. I, too, have an inkling of that God, and I, too, am terrified — terrified and fascinated, terrified and uplifted.

Tolstoi kept quiet about his knowledge. But that he had it no one who has some understanding of what was happening to him can doubt. Gorki glimpsed it in him. It shines strangely and darkly through his later conversations. It is the reason why he cared no more for his own miraculous writing. Yet it seems there are people who will, for their own comfort's sake, go on supposing that this Titan became a baby. After all, it is not comfortable to think out a thought about Tolstoi to the bitter end, any more than it is comfortable to think out an honest thought about Shakespeare. It is so much easier, so much less disturbing to think dishonest thoughts, and feel dishonest feelings. Shakespeare is 'serene' and Tolstoi pietistic at the last. God's in his heaven, all's right with the world. And the people who profess not to believe in God are just as cowardly as the rest. Shakespeare was bored and Tolstoi *gaga*, and what we haven't the courage to look at we can't possibly see.

But apparently it is impossible for some people to understand certain elemental realities. And because they cannot or will not understand these things, because they cannot admit (from vanity, or stupidity or cowardice) that there are more things in heaven and earth than are spoken of in their philosophy, it is inconceivable, strictly impossible, that they can understand either Shakespeare or Tolstoi or Whitman or Dostoevsky or Nietzsche or Tchehov or Melville – or any one of the great prophets of the modern consciousness, or life itself with which those prophets have wrestled until the going down of the sun. These silly little playboys – unless they begin to mend their ways and learn– will be condemned to pass to a dishonourable old age with nothing more accomplished than the experiencing 'an acute emotion before a Matisse,' of which one of them so rashly tells us. Oh, these 'acute emotions!' Oh, my acute emotions when I hear of them!

Well, to return. I had been saturating myself in

Tolstoi for days, every day marvelling more and more at, and more and more intimately revering the stature and the knowledge of that gigantic man. And as I made towards my Swiss resting-place, everything I saw and heard on the journey seemed to be part of *War and Peace*. When two Italian Swiss peasants in the railway-train called me in to umpire a dispute concerning the merits of the wine called Barbera, which they had evidently been looking upon while it was red, I felt like Pierre Bezuhov talking to Platon Karataev in the prisoners' hut. The very sunshine on the hills was part of Tolstoi's enchantment; and I found myself moving about, getting into trains and out again, accepting chance encounters, with an odd kind of submission, an unfamiliar acquiescence, as though I also had been bodily incorporated into the elemental scheme. I was playing a predestined part in the panorama of history of which Tolstoi was the demiurge.

I don't suppose it was wholly due to Tolstoi. It has been borne in upon me of late that our vital encounters are not fortuitous. One reads a book, one rejoins a friend, because one is prepared. Some subterranean travail has been going on, working our elements into a condition in which some new combination is inevitable. We are waiting for the spark which shall explode and re-order them. And in this condition we instinctively refuse all contacts which are less than decisive. Unconscious purpose drives us on to reject the accidental and penultimate. We are governed and we submit. As with men and women, so with books, for those at least to whom books are the impress of a living soul and not a pastime or a titillation. The mystery accumulating in ourselves is drawn towards a kindred mystery, by knowing which we shall know ourselves. That is the law.

So it has seemed in these last few days that I had never really read *War and Peace*. But now it was waiting for me and I for it: now for the first time, I lived it through and understood. It was part of me for ever. Uplifted with this knowledge, and with thoughts like these wheeling about my head, I made my way up the mountain to my Swiss resting-place, – one full of memories for me. I found, as I knew I should find, that I could bear all these memories and look them in the face. I was at peace.

And then a strange thing happened. On the next day another guest arrived, a man scarcely older than myself. We talked at tea.

'I've never been in Switzerland before,' he said.

'I thought everybody went to Switzerland,' said I.

'Every Englishman perhaps; but an Irishman doesn't believe in any mountains except the Macgillicuddy Reeks. And besides, there are only two European countries that attract me – Spain and Russia.'

'So you know Russia?'

'Yes, I know Russia pretty well. I lived for six months with Tolstoi at Yasnaia Poliana.'

Of course — I got my intelligence to work — it was quite possible. And yet, if he had said he had lived six months with Shakespeare, I should not have been more astonished, or more disturbed. My brain tells me that there are probably hundreds of men living to-day who have talked with Tolstoi. But whether it was that this was a man of my own generation, whose place I myself might have taken, or whether — as sometimes happens with me — I had been conversing so long with Tolstoi in the spirit that I could not imagine contact with him in the body, I was amazed and silent, brooding over the manifest predestination of this encounter also.

And, because of this sense that things would happen as they must, I found it impossible to ask him about what happened there, or what Tolstoi said and did. I waited. Later in the evening he gave an account of how he entered the house, and how he sat down to dinner. Tolstoi spoke to him suddenly.

'Are you a virgin?' he asked.

That was all. I was satisfied. Again I should not have guessed it; but I knew it must be so. 'Does he believe in God?' 'Are you a virgin?' The truly great are those who know the significance of elemental things.

(*October*, 1923.)

123

Novels and Thought-Adventures

IN MR. D. H. LAWRENCE'S LATEST novel, *Kangaroo*, he makes in his attractive, offhand way, a pronouncement about the art he is practising which is worth our best attention. 'Now a novel,' he says, 'is supposed to be a mere record of emotion-adventures, flounderings in feelings. We insist that a novel is, or should be, also a thought-adventure, if it is to be anything at all complete.'

That is a statement I like: first, because it compels me into a little thought-adventure of my own, making me think things over and out; and, second, because I am in essential agreement with what I believe it means. *Allons!* (as Mr. Lawrence would say) and let us embark on a little thought-adventure for ourselves.

Now I do not believe it can convincingly be made out that all novels which have a permanent place in our affections *are* thought-adventures. Take three of which I am particularly fond: *Robinson Crusoe*, *The Pickwick Papers*, and *The Ebb-Tide*. There is no perceptible thought-adventure in any of them. They are all records of adventure; but of adventure in the ordinary, straightforward sense. Robinson Crusoe, it is true, scratches his turnip-head quite hard after the apparation of the Devil; he enters up his blessings and his curses very neatly in a sort of ledger;

but the substance of his thinking does not amount to much. It is so unimportant that we can safely skip those pages. And of the other two stories it is even more true that they are chiefly the records of what happens *to* the characters, not of what happens *in* them. It's good enough: we are thrilled and delighted. After all, *le monde visible existe*. In it there are Champions of England who are knocked out in ten seconds, and cart-horses and people in railway-trains and crack footballers and falling leaves and crocodiles; and there is a kind of novel-writing which corresponds to their substantiality: novels in which we don't want to think or even to feel, but simply to watch. The world is full of a number of things. Praised be the Lord!

So Mr. Lawrence was not enunciating an absolute truth. Besides, there aren't any absolute truths. Any absolute worth twopence is a personal absolute: a promulgation of an imperious necessity felt by *me*. The depth and integrity of my feeling alone give it force and validity. If at a given point in the world's history there are a number of people who feel already, or after I have spoken discover that they feel, like me, then we may talk, quite provisionally, of an absolute. The human consciousness is making a move; it is going my way; I am the visible straw that shows how the wind is blowing.

Mr. Lawrence's statement is a personal and provisional absolute of this kind. 'This is the sort of novel we need nowadays' is what he is saying. And I agree; it seems to me that I have agreed for years. After all, when I read those three favourite novels of mine, I am always conscious that I am reading them as a sort of relaxation. I am amusing myself, just as I am amusing myself when I chuck stones into the sea. I like chucking stones into the sea; when I cease to like it, I shall know that I am growing old, and that it's time that I gave way. But chucking stones into the sea, though it has given me some blissful moments, is not my real job. Neither is reading *Robinson Crusoe*, or *The Pickwick Papers*, or *The Ebb-Tide*. The novels which it is my job to read are the novels which exert me completely; those which when I read, I feel that I am now going along my own pre-destined line, not doing fanciful and delightful little side-loops, or pausing to amuse myself by walking backwards on my hands. There is some place – I don't know where; perhaps if I did I should imme-diately start going somewhere else – to which I have to go. I make instinctively for the books that will help me on the way. I don't really enjoy them: they concern me much too deeply, I am far too much in-volved in them to enjoy them. I enjoy chucking stones; I don't enjoy climbing a mountain against time. But I *have* to climb the mountain; and I know that if I begin to spend more than a limited amount of time chucking stones, I shall be miserable. The world may be full of a number of things, and I will praise the Lord for it; but just now I can't afford to look too long at them. I have to get up that mountain somehow and have a glimpse of what is on the other side before the sun goes down.

Allons! therefore, by all means. I make for the books that will help me up that mountain. And they are the books that are the record of thought-adventure as well as emotion-adventure. Plato was the first writer who meant a great deal to *me*. Therefore I didn't enjoy him; I was altogether too much agitated. Then came the first novelist who caught me between wind and water. He was Stendhal. I was young then; and I was excited, as I always am excited, by a kind of mystery. I felt there was something more in him than he expressed, or could express; and I wanted to know what that something was. That, I have come to learn, is the chief sign that a novel is for *me*. And when I began excavating into Stendhal, I began to see what it was that held me. Stendhal, after his fashion, which is not my fashion, had stood up for life. He had tried to discover what life was, what could be done with it, what could be got out of it: and within his limitations he was absolutely honest. I learnt something of importance from him. Then came Dostoevsky. The

127

sense of mystery was overwhelming; I was knocked
flat and trampled on by *The Brothers Karamazov*. I
picked myself up and determined to find out what
Dostoevsky was trying to say; for that again, I knew,
had something to do with *me*. I began to unravel in
his books a thought-adventure of the dizziest, one
for which Stendhal had in part prepared me, but
which so far exceeded Stendhal's capacities, that they
cannot be compared. Dostoevsky remains for me the
ultimate outpost of the attempt at an intellectual discovery of life. Within his ambit he is supreme; he
carried the intellectual challenge to life to the bitter
end. And the end was bitter indeed. The intellectual
consciousness is *kaput!* Nothing to do but to wait
for a miracle.

Well, that was in the middle of the war, when every-
day events seemed to be proving in action that Dostoevsky was right. We had indeed reached an end.
Very good: let's nail the flag of the intellectual consciousness to the mast and go down imperturbable.
I was ready for melodramatic heroisms and frozen
ecstasies. The war, and the meaning of the war that
I read through Dostoevsky, had finished me. There
was nothing, except the chance of a miracle. You
can't shape your life on the expectation of a miracle.
So I gritted my teeth in a sort of cold intellectual
frenzy and said: There *is* nothing! And I took to
Tchehov, who is the great *artist* of the end: the man

who knew that all great writers had 'axes to grind' and he had none.

Well, there is no going on from Tchehov. We must just thank our lucky stars that an end should have been made as beautiful and humane as he made it: a Finis of which the intellectual consciousness can be proud.

   'Come, come, no time for lamentation now;
   Nor much more cause.'

But it was the end of the chapter; for me anyhow, for the Western world perhaps.

So there I stood, marking time. I didn't begin chucking stones into the sea; I wasn't in the least in the mood for that. I just stood there where the track ended, with a dry weariness in my heart, and wept.

But I wouldn't go back; I couldn't go back. I stood still. I saw Marcel Proust and James Joyce emerge. I examined them, for I am a top-heavy person who has to examine things. Essentially, from my point of view essentially, they are nothing. Landmarks, perhaps, to tell me twice again that the intellectual consciousness is utterly *kaput*. But I didn't want to be told that again, either elegantly or elaborately; I knew it long ago. What Tchehov had done sincerely and simply and perfectly, they were trying to do fashionably, elaborately and unnecessarily. It was a waste of time. Possibly it may be art. I know it is not the kind of art that deeply interests me. I am a detective by profession, and I can interest myself deliberately, in a professional kind of way, in anything. But neither Marcel Proust nor James Joyce interest *me*. There is more really profound thought-adventure in one of Tchehov's stories like *The Black Monk* than in all their work put together. They have talent, buckets of it, but talent – what's the use of talent except to help you to say something of importance for life?

So I brooded over Shakespeare, instead. There is plenty of thought-adventure there for anyone who will take the trouble to read the signs and symbols. Plenty of real thought-adventure, I mean: the thought that is not an abstract functioning in the void, but the index in the intellectual consciousness of life-adjustments that are taking place in the secret soul below. Shakespeare is the first of the moderns; the curve of his thought-adventure is the curve which all the great pioneers of the modern consciousness have had to follow. On a big scale or a little one you will find nearly all the creative minds of the first importance travelling the same path, a path which ends in the felt necessity of a new order of consciousness and of life. The Russian novelists, Tolstoy and Dostoevsky, brought us most consciously to the verge of this; but over in America, Melville and, above all, Whitman, their souls made pregnant by generations of contact with the elemental, with continent and ocean, were hinting at a new way.

Well, this new way isn't going to be easy. It's not easy for one who has breathed the air of the old European tradition to say Good-bye to the intellectual consciousness and take the plunge into nothingness, even though he knows it necessary and can watch with his own eyes the fabric of Europe settling into decay. It isn't going to be easy at all. All the more reason therefore to look for help where we can get it. All the more reason why, deliberately adjusting our standards to our needs, we should demand that our books — and our books nowadays are bound to be novels — should be not only emotion-adventures but thought-adventures also. We can't spend our time chucking stones into the sea; we can't even afford the minutes necessary to smile at Mr. George Moore preening himself over a collogue with Mr. Granville Barker in *The Fortnightly Review*. Chucking stones into the sea is a much better occupation than that, anyhow.

It is because we are where we are that the novel of thought-adventure is necessary. All the rest, just now, is fiddling while Rome is burning. It may be a shortcoming of mine, but I can't listen: this twiddling fiddling makes me angry. I want to get on. There's that mountain still to be climbed; and I've spent so many years already trying to get up it from the wrong side. All the thought-adventure possible that way has been done, done superlatively. Now we need someone who will spy out a new path from another side that will take us beyond the blank wall to which the old European tradition has been leading since the Renaissance.

And it seems to me — my personal and provisional absolute again — that only the novelist who has a sense of this necessity in which we are involved can do any really vital work to-day. The other kind of novel-writing exists, but just now it is bound to be trivial and nugatory. The sense of security essential to its perfect flowering isn't there, and it's no use pretending it is. Either the novelist is aware of the actual condition of the human consciousness and of the world — for this bankruptcy which may have been difficult to discern as a potentiality fifty or a hundred years ago, is now a visible reality — and if he is aware of it his work must be a thought-adventure; or he is blind to it, and then his blindness to a thing so palpable argues him negligible.

Not that I want the Old Guard to change. What they have done well, let them go on doing well. More power to their elbows! But the Young Guard can't follow them. It only makes an unholy mess of it when it tries. Its business is to get on with its own job; and if the Old Guard can't understand what it's up to, well, that can't be helped, and we bear them no grudge provided that they don't go asking us for things we can't give. And, after all, we aren't asking to be understood by our elders, but by our contemporaries. The generation for whom the war was a vital and crucial part of their life-experience is bound to be generically different from the older generation who managed to pass it by on the other side. Some of the younger generation also managed to do that; and between them and us the gulf is deeper, far deeper.

(*October*, 1923.)

More about Romanticism

THOSE OF MY READERS WHO RE-
member the hurried defence of Romanticism I
lately made will be pleased to learn that I have found
a real opponent in Mr. T. S. Eliot, the gifted editor
of *The Criterion*.

I at least am glad of the encounter. I am not by
inclination provocative; and when I wrote on Romanticism I was not engaged in trailing my coat, or asking for a fight for the fun of the thing. I felt that if
my challenge called forth a reply worth replying to,
we might manage to make a further stage in our
voyage of discovery. Perhaps we shall.

The debate, I profoundly believe, is concerned with
fundamentals. But, since it was begun casually and
upon a trivial occasion, it is as well to clear my own
decks of irrelevant top-hamper. The definite propositions which I asserted or implied were (1) that I
am a Romantic; (2) that the essential attitude of
Romanticism is an obedience to the inner voice,
whereas Classicism consisted in obedience to an external spiritual authority; (3) that the tradition of
English literature and of English spiritual life in
general is Romantic. These were my original asser-
tions. The first of these propositions is of no great
concern to anybody, except in so far as it gives some
guarantee that the debate is of much more than

academic interest to me: I am engaged in defending not my preferences but my convictions.

There was, however, a further proposition which was not definitely asserted, but implied. I have been and am engaged (among other things) in attacking not classicists, but pseudo-classicists. I deny neither the fact nor the worth of Classicism, in its place, just as I do not deny the fact or the worth of the Catholic Church, in its place. I do not regard Classicism and Romanticism as two diametrically opposed and mutually exclusive truths. As intellectual truths, as Platonic archetypes stored up in the realm of the incorruptible Idea, I have no doubt they co-exist. As truths, as historical facts, they suffer one another; but as active beliefs they are utterly opposed. That is to say, a man who has reached a condition of sufficient spiritual maturity to be a Classicist or a Romantic, must be one or the other. He cannot be both; and he cannot be neither. To be neither is to *be* nothing. And there is a further implied assertion in the shape of an implicit answer to the question: Which should a man be at this point of time? The answer is : A Romantic.

It seems to me that the whole controversy can best be advanced, not by my arguing these original propositions of mine in the order of their assertion or by attempting to confute the criticisms of them made to some extent *en passant* by Mr. T. S. Eliot in *The*

Criterion. The sooner the accidental and contingent elements are eliminated from this debate the better; for then we shall more quickly have a glimpse of the real nature of the issues that are involved. I shall therefore try to restate the whole of my position in such a way that all my original propositions are reasserted as members of an organic whole.

Romanticism and Classicism are perennial modes of the human spirit. They have existed in all times and in all places. The Catholic Church, which is essentially classical, has contained without bursting a good many romantic movements; and Christianity itself, which is essentially romantic, has endured the imperial classicism of the Roman Church without being altogether destroyed. And long before Christianity and far outside the Western world, the opposition in other names and forms, has surely existed. It is indeed impossible to conceive the human spirit as operant save in one or other of these modes. The labels are of to-day or yesterday; but the realities are of all time. The history of the human soul is the story of romanticisms organized into classicisms, and classicisms rebelled against and defeated by romanticisms.

But in this history of the human soul there are epochs. We choose the one nearest to us for two excellent reasons: we know most about it, and we are ourselves involved in it. This epoch manifestly begins with the Renaissance and the Reformation. The Renaissance was the rebellion of a great Romanticism against a secular Classicism. The individual asserted himself against the external spiritual authority, consolidated and actual throughout the Middle Ages, of the Roman Church; he vindicated his right to stand or fall by his own experience, to explore the universe for himself. That is the beginning of modern Romanticism: Shakespeare is its prophetic voice, modern as no other voice of the past is modern, valid, completely valid, until this epoch of man's spiritual history shall end: Romantic through and through, and Romantic to the very verge of human experience.

Man, at the Renaissance, vindicated his right to explore the universe for himself, and to stand or fall by his own experience of it. From that moment onwards generations of men began to go through the slow process of rediscovering for themselves truths which a representative and prophetic man like Shakespeare had discovered in himself and symbolically uttered. First and foremost, that there are two universes to explore: without and within, the external and the internal world. The exploration of the external world was at first more exciting: but by the time Dampier and Anson had girdled the globe, the more chilly discovery of Galileo had begun to penetrate. The earth was parochial; the inhabitants thereof positively trivial. The first fine frenzy of Goddestruction cooled to an uneasy suspicion that a worse than the comer in dyed garments from Bozra had been imperceptibly enthroned – Necessity. The external world was uncomfortably revealed as a world of law, but without a bearded law-giver. Voltaire cachinnated over the spectacle; Rousseau refused to believe in it. While Diderot in his Encyclopædia went on with the task of charting the external world, Jean-Jacques turned his back on it, looked at the internal world, and made the mistake of propounding its fundamental truth in terms of the external world to which it did not apply. 'Man is born free; he is everywhere in chains.' That was Romantic in the limited modern sense. What Rousseau meant to say – or at least what Rousseau ought to have said – was: 'Man *is* free; and he is everywhere subject to necessity.' That might have been less dramatic and less moving; some might say it would have been less Romantic, and more true.

But, as a matter of fact, though it is seldom recognized, there are two degrees in Romanticism. The name is generally confined to the more elementary of the two; the more advanced has no name at all, apparently because it has not yet been clearly isolated and distinguished. And no thoroughgoing anatomy of Romanticism is possible at all unless it is referred to the fundamental paradox of human existence and human knowledge. This paradox, acute at various stages in the recorded history of the human soul, became peremptory at the Renaissance, when man claimed once more his full and indefeasible freedom to explore the universe. It has remained peremptory, though sometimes its urgency has been concealed, ever since.

The paradox is this: as man seeks to know the universe, he finds outside him a realm of necessity and within him a realm of freedom; and he finds, moreover, that to know the external world as a world of necessity is the necessary condition of knowing it at all, and likewise that to know the internal world as a world of freedom is the necessary condition of knowing it at all. These knowledges are both alike knowledge; yet they are different in kind and contradictory in content. The two degrees of Romanticism correspond to the two degrees of awareness of this paradox. The more elementary phase is marked by a passionate vindication of the freedom of the self, of which there is immediate knowledge. The primary Romantic, as we may call him, is aware of the realm of necessity hardly more than as a menace against which he is in instant rebellion. He retires defiantly into the fortress of the ego, and proclaims that the world wherein his felt sovereignty and freedom no longer hold is a world of illusion. He solves the mystery of the cosmos by an appeal to his immediate experience, and unites by proclamation the kingdom of necessity to his own kingdom of freedom. The warrant for this proclamation is an act of what is generally called mystical perception.

Now the question arises: What validity and scope are to be attached to this mystical perception? It is real enough — only fools presume to doubt its reality. But whereas the primary romantic claims for it a comprehensive ontological truth, as a revelation of the actual structure of the universe; the secondary romantic does not. It seems to him dangerous, one-sided and untrue to dismiss the external world as a world of illusion; and he knows that it is impossible to live by these moments of mystical apprehension, and that they can only be maintained at the cost of a certain spiritual duplicity: on the other hand, he knows their reality. So he regards them as indications, prophetic monitions, of some as yet undeveloped faculty of apprehension in the human mind, and of some underlying reality with which, lacking that faculty, the human mind cannot permanently establish contact. Thus he comes to regard the fundamental paradox not as an insoluble contradiction in the nature of reality, but as a congenital limitation of human vision. Humanity, being what it is and where it is, is compelled to consider its universe under the categories of without and within, and of necessity and freedom. But the reality of that universe is truly apprehended under neither of these categories. And, although it is foolish to attempt even by way of parable a description of the reality of the universe, in order to make a tenuous thought more tangible we may risk saying that the reality might be imagined as an organic and living whole: in which there would be necessity and freedom, but the necessity would not be the necessity of intellectual apprehension, and the freedom other than the freedom of which I am immediately conscious in myself.

This rejection of a one-sided and egocentric solution of the paradox of freedom and necessity, which distinguishes those whom I have called 'secondary' Romantics, does not in itself offer a solution. But it hints at the way by which a solution might be found. If the human consciousness is by nature incapable of apprehending the world of its experience save under contradictory categories, then we must wait for a change in the very nature of human consciousness. To some minds, perhaps to most minds, such a notion will seem fantastic and incredible. To others, for example, to those who read anthropology as the record of the reality of the human soul, the notion will be neither fantastic nor incredible. And certainly this notion possessed the three of the greatest creative minds of the literature which is truly modern. It was the final word of Shakespeare, of Tolstoi, and of Dostoevsky. To make such an assertion *sans phrase*, especially in the case of the first member of the trinity, is painful to me as a literary critic; but the justification of my assertion would fill more than a volume.

I hope I have at least succeeded in sketching out a scheme within which the question of Romanticism must be placed in order that its importance may be seen and its implications appreciated. If I have, and if the scheme is accepted, then it seems to me to follow immediately that the real question to be answered in regard to any Romanticism at any time, is not whether Romanticism is true, but whether it is necessary or expedient at a particular stage in the secular adventure of the human soul. Mr. Eliot has asked, 'Is it *right?*' And thereby, I think, to some extent, showed that even he was not wholly aware of the nature of the problem. For 'right' may mean 'true,' or it may mean 'expedient': it may be a judgment of propositions or of conduct. And it seemed to me that Mr. Eliot had not yet formed a clear notion of which 'rightness' he was asking for.

Of course, it is possible, though I cannot believe it very probable, that Mr. Eliot holds that in all times and in all places Romanticism is untrue and inexpedient. It would be a strange position for a student of anthropology and an admirer of Elizabethan literature. And, if my scheme is accepted, the judgment that Romanticism is untrue will appear as a judgment without import, and the judgment that it is always inexpedient nothing less than the utterance of a conservatism that, were it possible, would have held humanity fast in the protozoic slime.

Nor is it of any avail for the classicist to appeal to the tradition. The tradition is, in the main, the organization and consolidation of many romanticisms, just as the Catholic Church was the organization and consolidation of the great romanticism of Christ. That organization began in the fifteenth and sixteenth centuries to exercise a deathly constraint on the adventuring human soul: and there was rebellion against it. The rebellion was easiest and most complete in these islands. England shed the Roman Church as easily as a snake its skin; other countries went through agonies in the effort to rid themselves of it, as though it were the shirt of Nessus. And the cause of the difference in these reactions, as I understand them, was that the Roman Church had never achieved an essential hold upon the English mind and soul. The English are a nation of individualists *par excellence;* they do not have to organize their romanticism, they simply are romantic. Not romantic to the exclusion of every classicism, of course, — there are no pure cases of romanticism save in the madhouse, or of classicism save in the museums — but in the sense that their instinctive bias is towards the fullest individual freedom. There will never be any life and death struggles between classicism and

romanticism in England: there are no real opponents for romanticism to battle with. And even Mr.
Eliot, the author of *The Waste Land*, the champion
of *Ulysses*, is not a true-blue classicist, however much
he might like to be. Anatole France, in spite of
all his romantic humanitarianism, is a classicist
in his bones; an English Tory is quite another
thing.

Not that I attach much importance to this question
of our national peculiarities as an evidence of the
value of Romanticism, though I do find much significance in the fact that our greatest national poet –
who is, indeed, our only national poet – is also the
greatest and profoundest of all literary Romantics.
And I agree with Mr. Eliot that a proposition is not
necessarily true because it is English. But it seems
to me indubitable, first, that something more fundamental than a proposition is in question, and, second,
that this fundamental thing is of such a nature that
to discuss whether it is, in itself, right or wrong, is
a misapplication of energy. And if these arguments
are granted, then the fact that Romanticism is a
natural aptitude of the English soul begins to have
an importance. For if, as I believe, it is possible that
an advance towards a new phase of consciousness
may be begun, and if, as seems to me obvious, it can
be achieved only by a new Romanticism, then the
fact that the soul of England is an *anima naturaliter*

romantica points to the likelihood that England has still a great part to play in the immediate future of mankind. For English Romanticism is Romanticism with a difference. It is not an intellectual gymnastic or a melodramatic gesture, as it has been in Latin countries; it is on the contrary a practical and experimental Romanticism. It retains some kind of contact with the deep springs of life; it does not confuse the kingdom of necessity with the kingdom of freedom; it is not revolutionary or catastrophic; it learns by experience; it has a vast accumulation of instinctive wisdom.

It is, however, no part of my present purpose to sing the praises of England, though it is part of my creed that England has a mission; because I believe that the real continuity of the Western consciousness is preserved in her alone. While the great effort of Russia symbolized in Tolstoi and Dostoevsky has ended in disintegration, and the great effort of America symbolized in Whitman and Melville has ended in a mechanical stagnation, England is still living, still organically evolving. And she has no need of the restraining influences of a classicism that has no root in the English soul. In the name of a kindred classicism Ben Jonson said of Shakespeare: *Sufflaminandus erat:* 'Some one ought to have put the brake on him.' But Shakespeare knew better, even though his knowledge was instinctive; he knew

better, precisely because his knowledge was instinctive: and he went his way.

Perhaps it will seem unpleasantly insular that I
should claim for English romanticism a privilege of
relative immunity from romantic error. Yet the fact
seems to me incontrovertible. From what the deep-
rooted English instinct for individual freedom comes
I do not know: it exists, and I accept it and rejoice in
it. For it seems to me that it is because this sense of
the spiritual autonomy of the individual really exists
in England, that the Englishman has no temptation
to project this freedom into a realm where it has no
validity. It is not an intoxicating novelty to him; it
has become, during the centuries, a primary function
of his being: and the great equivoque of Rousseau
has had, and always will have, singularly little dominion over him. Rousseau, I believe, spoke in parables: it is dangerous to speak to the Latin mind in
parables; because the Latin mind, which craves for
external authority, cannot help turning parables into
dogmas. Just as in the greater matter Rome organized Christianity, so in the lesser France organized –
that is, endeavoured to translate into rigid political
terms, Rousseau's proclamation of the spiritual freedom of man. Such an effort of translation would instinctively be felt by the English soul to be fallacious:
the freedom of one world cannot be transposed into

a freedom of another world. It may be insular prejudice; but I cannot imagine the English nation, even if it were placed in the same circumstances of danger, behaving with the preposterous mechanical rigidity that France is now displaying in European affairs. I regard such behaviour as a profound offence against life, and I discern its origin in an essential insecurity in the French soul. It cannot possess itself in patience and repose on its own inward strength; it must have the outward show of power in order to believe that it has power at all.

That is to say that, in its political manifestations, classicism, as a principle to-day, is rigid and inflexible; it deliberately divorces itself from instinct, and life is, after all, in the main an affair of instinct. And, at this present time, when the rapid disintegration of European institutions seems to be inevitable, when calculation is a reed that breaks in a man's hand, and logic appears an unusually fantastic disguise for reality, the nation which relies most completely upon instinct and is quickest to divest itself of the mechanics of authority is the nation which holds the greatest promise for the future.

Ah, but this 'reliance upon instinct' — is it anything, asks Mr. Eliot, but the old principle of anarchy: To do what you like? Well, I admit that it is not easy to *define* the difference; and since a classicist must believe that nothing really exists that cannot be defined, and indeed that things *are* in virtue of their definitions, it is difficult for me to meet him here. Yes, of course, to rely upon instinct is, in a sense, to do what you like. And perhaps (though I do not believe it) to do what you like may seem rather easy to Mr. Eliot. To me, on the contrary, it seems the hardest thing in the world. For to know what you really like means to know what you really are; and that is a matter of painful experience and slow exploration. To discover that within myself which I *must* obey, to gain some awareness of the law which operates in the organic whole of the internal world, to feel this internal world as an organic whole working out its own destiny according to some secret vital principle, to know which acts and utterances are a liberation from obstacles and an accession of strength, to acknowledge secret loyalties which one cannot deny without impoverishment and starvation, — this is to possess one's soul indeed, and it is not easy either to do or to explain. And yet, I believe that it can be done without deceiving oneself; and I also believe that we have the faculty of recognizing instantly when another has achieved this consummation.

And when this consummation is achieved, a man is free; he is sovereign of his own inward world, and, kinglike, he can do no wrong. He is also obedient, for in any true exploration of the self, he must encounter that which is greater than himself; he also, no less than the classicist, submits to authority, but the authority is discovered by his own free act and recognized by his own free will. He surrenders his personal, vain, and exclusive *ego* and finds himself.

I might go on trying to describe this process for pages, without bringing one atom more conviction to those who find it incredible. It seems to me that this is one of the things which you either know or don't know; and that it is impossible to build a bridge between those two conditions. But I maintain that a complete romanticism demands a new discipline of the soul. Whether this discipline appears like anarchy to those who have no inkling of it—as indeed I suppose it must appear – seems to me of no great moment. I should like to be able to convince my sincere opponents; but I fear the ability is not in me.

Instead, I will try to sum up certain of my chief contentions. Ethically, Romanticism is an attempt to solve the problem of conduct by an exploration of the internal world. If this exploration is complete it will result in an immediate knowledge of what I may and may not do. The implication of the certainty of this knowledge is that at some point in this non-intellectual exploration of the self a contact is established between the finite soul and the infinite soul of which it is a manifestation. This mystical implication is borne out by the felt quality and validity of certain crucial experiences. But it is not necessary to insist upon this, and in this exposition I have avoided doing so.

Nevertheless, some sense of this implication is essential to a real romantic ; it helps to determine his attitude and to shape his belief that there is an underlying harmony in the external universe, of which he may have partial and momentary premonitions. In virtue of these he may regard the perceived nature of the external universe as an illusion. But this form of romanticism is incomplete. The more resolute romantic accepts the reality of the external universe, and finds the cause of its contradiction with the internal world—a contradiction theologically expressed as the opposition of free-will and necessity – in a limitation of the human consciousness. He believes that the human consciousness has not yet reached the point in its own development where it is capable of truly apprehending reality; such a change he believes to be inevitable, and towards such a change he strives.

This, as I see it, is the central essence of a true romanticism; and it seems to me obvious that the attitude is so fundamental that it must govern or at least influence every manifestation of the man who believes in it. In other words, a true romanticism necessitates a new theology, a new ethic, and a new politic. It would be mere foolishness on my part to try to indicate, by more than the passing hints I have given, the nature of these. Honestly, I do not know; to try to discover them in the course of an elaborate exposition would need many volumes, and I should run the danger of trying to organize a new romanticism into a new classicism, and of losing contact with the source. Sufficient for the day are the necessities thereof; and for the rest, *solvatur vivendo*.

(*November*, 1923.)

On Being Inhuman

SOMEONE HAS WRITTEN TO ME AND called me 'damnably inhuman.' It is not the first time this has happened; in fact, the accusation has been hurled at me periodically ever since I was old enough to have accusations hurled at me at all. For some reason I don't resent it as much as I used to. Nevertheless, just for a moment, I was staggered. I hadn't expected it. Somehow I had come to believe that I had become more human. It was, apparently, another delusion.

Well, it can't be helped. Instead of making frenzied exertions, as I would have done years ago, to prove that so far from being inhuman, I am really human – all too human, nowadays I am inclined to accept the epithet – at least to hold it in my hands for a while, in order that I may know what it means. My correspondent was not very helpful. '(Incidentally, you are damnably inhuman.)' In brackets, just like that, without a hint of why or how.

There must be something in it. The epithet wouldn't have stuck to me all the days of my life, if there wasn't. Even the fact that I feel no more impulse to defend myself against the charge – unless, perhaps, this is going to develop into a defence – seems to indicate that I feel somewhere within me that no defence is possible.

Yes, I suppose I am oddly detached from life. I have very few friends; and those I have have sometimes seemed none too sure of me: apparently they have felt that I am not quite solid, and that if they began to look upon me as a fixed star in their universes I might take the first opportunity to slip out of the sky. Moreover, I like to be solitary; there are moments when even the contacts I chiefly prize are intolerable to me, and I feel that not to be alone — not to be utterly and entirely alone, with nothing but my secret soul for company — would be to die. And again I shun new contacts: either they will touch me deeply — and why should I invite disturbances? — or they will touch me not at all — and why should I spend myself in vain? The men and women I know, yes, they are precious to me. I have proved them; they have come through the fiery trial of disbelieving in me, of finding me treacherous, even of imagining me diabolical, and, in spite of everything, I exist for them; they even seem to understand that it was necessary for me to have appeared to fail them utterly, just as I understand that it was necessary for me that they should have ceased to believe in me. A man in search of his soul has to be stripped naked; he clings in terror and desperation to his friends' belief in him: that spar also has to be torn from the hands of the drowning man. He must be suffered to cheat himself no more; he cannot exist simply because others believe he exists. He must exist in his own right, or not at all. Therefore the spar must be torn from his hands, and he must drown.

Well, then he drowns indeed. The great dark waters cover him, and the last spark seems to die. Yet something remains, some infinitesimal atom of the unquenchable – and that is he. With it, by virtue of it alone, he battles painfully to the surface of the waters and the divine light of day. What does it matter now *who* believes in him? Why should he waste his breath any more in declaring that he is he? He knows it, once for all, and that is enough. Though the world deny and his nearest still doubt, he must go his way. For he exists, and death hath no more dominion over him. He may die many times again, if it lie in his destiny; and he will die the mortal death which is the appointed end: but he knows the secret in his soul, and the secret is the mystery of death.

And now he knows why he was afraid; now he knows why he clutched so desperately at his friends' belief in him: simply that he was afraid of death. 'Who will save me from the terror of this death?' had been his secret cry, though he did not utter it. This death in a thousand unrecognizable forms, light as air and heavy as doom itself – from fear of the lifted eyebrow of the socially secure to the deep acknowledgment within himself that there might be a soul finer, greater, truer than his own. Little deaths, big deaths; but all partaking in their essence of the one solemn and eternal mystery of Death, never to be conquered save by the soul's submission to it, out of which alone rises the unshaken certainty: *Non omnis moriar*.

Inhuman still? Well, it may be; indeed it must be: but inhuman not in the same way. Inhuman, not because of non-existence any more, but in virtue of existence itself. Determined, secure, resolute, ruthless – something of all these perhaps, yet not one of them. They are all too brilliant, too conscious, too hard. Let us rather say simply, gathered, as a runner is gathered to run. Yet even that is too much: for the runner runs to a visible goal, and he to an invisible. No, let it be simply gathered: wary, flexible, alert, and self-contained.

Inhuman still? Because there is a purpose, though he does not know it, and a goal, though he cannot see it; and he must not turn aside. Though the purpose and the goal be unknown, what is known is every deviation from the path that leads toward it; and the knowledge of deviation is unbearable: it is a sense of constriction, a feeling of suffocation. For there is only one freedom – to have the personal turned away into impersonality, and to be free to follow the instinctive destiny that is the great source of our selves.

And yet not free *to* follow it; free rather, by following it, free by allowing that point of inextinguishable life which was so hard to discover and so desperately attained, to grow, to take control, to lead, to explore.

To explore — that is the word which returns and returns again. Life is an exploration of the unknown. But no longer as those explorations which he knew in his youth, when the mind said to him: 'This you have not tasted; this you have not done,' but an exploration wherein he does not know what he will encounter, wherein at the same time he explores the world within and the world without. For he knows himself now by what he will do, because he can do only that which it is permitted to him to do — that which he must do.

It is not easy to explain — this new security. 'If he could tell me in three words,' writes some one, ' what he is confident *about*.' He is not confident about anything: simply he is confident. About himself?

'Well, well, this word myself has many meanings.'

Confident about himself, if the self has all its old personal meaning burned away: if it is no longer something which he possesses, but which possesses him. Confident because he has found a master whom he must obey, who says unto him 'Do this and he doeth it.' Confident because he has acknowledged a destiny of which the end and process are unknown; confident because they are unknown: because everything matters and nothing matters, because he does not care and cares infinitely, because he loves men dearly and loves them not at all, because he is bound and free, waiting and not anxious, himself and not himself.

Not a very satisfying answer that, though there are more than three words to it. So let us try again, with that precious word ' exploration ' to help us. His is then the confidence of one embarked on a voyage of discovery. He has reached the end of all the old knowledge, the burden of which was grievous to him so long, and now miraculously, against all hope, he finds himself at the edge of an unknown sea; if it was ever charted, even the memory has been forgotten. And it seems to him miraculous that suddenly in the universe he knew, whose bounds had pressed like prison bars upon him, should shine the dark gleam of these uncharted waters. So long ago he gave up hope, now they lave his very feet.

And he who so many years chafed against the walls of existence and sought to escape into he knew not what unutterable realm of perfect beauty and perfect truth and perfect love, and found only the bitter bread of emptiness and desolation for his pains, has suddenly wakened as from a dream, not into knowledge of a harmony which may or may not be, but into the knowledge that if it is it is not to be found that way. And somehow it does not matter whether there is or is not a harmony that we can apprehend.

157

If we look for it we look in vain, for to look for it is a proof of discord and division in ourselves; but if we find the harmony in ourselves we do not need the harmony without. Instead, we know there is a purpose, of which we may be the forerunners. Therefore we strip for the race.

Inhuman, therefore — let me freely admit it — in a sense; in the sense that one cannot be bound any more by personal bonds. There is no more *I* on which they may take hold. Nevertheless, it is not by our own deliberate and conscious will that we are thus stripped. We reawaken slowly to the knowledge that we *are* separate and that we have a destiny to fulfil. It is not our doing: if it were, we could not believe in it, or trust it, or act by it. If we are inhuman therefore it is not our fault. A servant of life cannot return to a private capacity.

(*November*, 1923.)

Literature and Religion

WHAT IS RELIGION? IT IS A THING at once so abstract and so intimate, so indefinite and yet so real, that only a personal definition can avail, and even a personal definition cannot be produced at the sound of a trumpet. It needs a preliminary, tentative self-examination, and an endeavour to impose upon shapeless feelings a form against which they may rebel. Nevertheless, we must make a beginning.

Religion, let us say, is the sense in the human soul of a binding relation between itself and God. A definition with two vital and ultimate terms undefined, perhaps indefinable! For what is the human soul? And what is God? My soul is my self, the ultimate, irreducible I, the dark spring of living water within me on which my life depends, an essence not to be apprehended by my mind, for my mind is only a partial manifestation of it – a living spirit whose nature can be uttered only in the tremendous and mysterious words of Jehovah: I AM THAT I AM. The old falsity of the *Cogito, ergo sum* is far away from us now; for we know, as our minds cannot know, that it is untrue. Not *Cogito, ergo sum* is the mark of the soul, but *Sum, ergo cogito*. My soul is my profound, unutterable being, that manifests in thought, in feeling, in act, and above all in life that comprehends all three. My consciousness of my own freedom is my consciousness of my soul.

And what is God? Shall we say: That greater I AM to which my own I AM acknowledges a binding relation. The logician will say that we are burking definition. 'Read your sentence again now' – I seem to hear his laugh – ' " Religion is the sense in the human soul of a binding relation between itself and – that to which it has a binding relation." Ha, ha, ha!' And yet, somehow, we are not disturbed. We did not imagine, when we began, that logic would have much help for us. Let it solve the mysteries of its own tremendous problems, let it master the secret of Quanta; or let it admit that the structure of the universe is non-rational. And if the structure of the macrocosm be non-rational, the structure of the microcosm is assuredly also beyond reason. Beyond reason, without a doubt, is our initial certainty that the living soul exists. Will the logician challenge it in the name of reason? Whether he challenge it or not, we must go our way; we must be loyal to our certainties.

Perhaps, precisely because this binding relation of the human soul to that which is beyond it appears to us unequivocally to exist, we can best approach the nature of God, in deliberate independence of the laws of logic, from the immediately apprehended nature of the soul. The point at which the nature of the soul rises nearest to the light of the intellectual day is in our consciousness of the indefeasible freedom of the living self. Without that consciousness, we die, and if we deny it with our minds, we nevertheless accept it with that which is deeper than our minds, for unless we accept it, there remains to us nothing to deny it with. We *must*, therefore, acknowledge our freedom; and that of which we acknowledge the freedom is our soul.

We begin, then, with this: our immediate apprehension of the soul as the subject of the freedom which we know is ours. And this same immediate apprehension tells us more. Though our consciousness of the freedom of our soul remains unimpaired, there are certain things we cannot do; and these certain things are not such as are forbidden by the nature of the external world, wherein we freely admit necessity, but such as within ourselves we feel at the same moment that we are free to do and bound not to do, or free not to do and bound to do. In theological language, we are confronted with the mystery of conscience; but the word 'conscience,' worn thin, like most theological terms, by centuries of disputation and casuistry, will no longer hold what it must contain. The immediate experience to which, in the language of Christian psychology, the word 'conscience' corresponds is in itself as much positive as negative. The 'Thou shalt' is at least as frequent as the 'Thou shalt not.'

What we feel in ourselves is this. In the heart of an essential freedom which is ours, which we have called the freedom of the soul, there is a sense of inner obligation to obey the command of something deeper even than the soul itself. Of our souls we are, save in sleep, continually aware; the consciousness of our fundamental freedom never abandons us. But the voice of this inner command is intermittent; it may be silent for days and months together, when there remains only the sense of our obligation to obey it when it is audible. Perhaps the inward reality of this experience has never been more truly expressed than by the lines of the French poet Paul Claudel, describing his own religious conversion.

'J'ai fui partout; partout j'ai retrouvé la loi,
  Quelquechose en moi qui soit plus moi-même qui moi.'

For this voice when it sounds, sounds to us as the voice of the innermost I; this law is, indeed, more myself than I. And our obedience to it is not an abrogation of our soul's freedom, but a consummation of it. Our consciousness of this command is the deepest point of our knowledge of our own identity. Here we touch the very quick of being, the secret core where self passes into not-self and is born as self once more; this and none other is the meeting-place

162

of the soul and God, the moment of contact and fusion between the I AM that is within and the I AM that is beyond – beyond, because we know it as exceeding the soul's capacity, and apprehend it immediately as infinite. It is the ocean wherein we drown and the fount whence our life springs. And at the point in our exploration of the soul's reality where we see the necessary and living identity of personality and impersonality, we comprehend quite simply the meaning of Christ's mystical saying, 'He that loseth his life shall save it,' for the essential life of the soul consists in a losing of the soul for its own renewal.

The sense of this inward motion, the consciousness of this binding relation between the two I AM's, is what I understand by the word 'religion.' It may be formulated, I imagine, in a thousand different ways and articulated in a thousand different systems; but the formulation in the sayings of Christ is one, I believe, which can never be superseded. It is simple, naked, and essential, and it touches the heart of the mystery more nearly than any formulation of which written record remains to us.

If, therefore, as I believe, religion is the fundamental reality of the human soul; if the consciousness of the soul itself demands for its very existence the consciousness of God; if the lesser I AM can only be in virtue of the greater I AM from which it draws its life – then literature, which is a manifestation of that same soul whose deepest anatomy is contained in religion, must inevitably be knit up with, be indissolubly bound to, religion. There is no escape. Religion and Literature are branches of the same everlasting root.

No doubt, in so far as each may depart far from its living centre, the indissoluble bond between them may sometimes be hard to discern. The vital motion of religion becomes petrified into dogmas and ceremonies; the vital motion of literature is ossified into forms and canons; and between these empty husks the connection is invisible and non-existent, precisely because it is a connection between the living essences. When literature becomes a parlour-game and religion a church-mummery, they are alike only in their deadness. But between the literature that is real and the religion that is real the bond is close and unbreakable.

So close and unbreakable, I could almost believe, that in those periods of human history when religion is at once superbly organized and close to its own living centre, the creative impulse of literature might well be enfeebled because the need it satisfies is less urgent. Perhaps the coincidence of the time when the spiritual and temporal realities of the Christian Church seemed identical and the time when Western literature was moribund is not in the least fortuitous; and it may be that the decay of dogmatic religion, because of its failure to express the religious reality and satisfy the religious needs of the soul, is a necessary condition in order that literature may truly grow and flourish. It may be that the moment comes when the finest and most sensitive minds are compelled to be of the Church, but not in it; when, precisely because they are profoundly religious, they are bound to work in complete independence of what passes for religion in their day.

Certain it is that since the Renaissance literature and religion in the West appear at the first sight to have gone their separate ways, so that the mere attempt to establish and make visible what seems to some a self-evident connection between the two realities appears to others either an endeavour to undermine the foundations of religion or a manifest blasphemy against the sacrosanct conception of 'art.' Yet, surely, these fears are purblind. One may surely admit, even while he feels that a systematized belief is necessary, that religion is more than systematized belief; and another may surely admit, even while he feels that 'art' is necessary, that literature is something more than 'art.'

Of course, no man is a writer simply because he has a soul. He needs also the gift of expression, the faculty of using words creatively so that they compel his readers to think and to feel and to see as he desires them to think and feel and see. And we may, if we choose, completely isolate this faculty from all others with which it may have an organic connection, and declare that this and this alone constitutes the essence of literature. But this beginning will not take us far; we find, very soon, that by this act of isolation we have killed the living object of our inquiry, having severed it from its root. To consider this maimed and desiccated literature is like trying to apprehend the nature of flowers by contemplating those plucked and rootless blossoms which German children stick in the turf of a grave. They droop and wither while we look at them.

We cannot *know* a work of literature except as a manifestation of the rhythm of the soul of the man who created it. If we stop short of that, our understanding is incomplete. We may enjoy, we may be thrilled, we may imagine that we are appreciating some absolute æsthetic perfection; but we are only sensationalists. We cannot know its essence and its individuality. For, if we take this consideration of a work of literature as a thing-in-itself at its highest, as an appreciation of some absolute æsthetic perfection, two imperious obstacles bar the way to a full understanding: first, the fact that æsthetic perfection must be absolute, and that all writings which possess it, considered from this angle, are the same, because there can be no difference in the quality of an absolute perfection; and, second, that in fact hardly one of the works of literature which, by the consensus of generations, are reckoned great, possesses this quality of æsthetic perfection. Shakespeare, Tolstoy, Dickens, Dostoevsky, Keats, Stendhal, Wordsworth, Whitman, Carlyle, Balzac – not one in a hundred of the works of these masters can, by the wildest flight of imagination, be called æsthetically perfect. They have style, they have individuality, they have life; they move us profoundly, disturb and delight us; but to call what we feel an æsthetic emotion, or that in them to which we respond an æsthetic perfection, would be a wanton misuse of language.

The great writer has to be two things. He has to be a writer; to have the gift of compulsive language, of words that live and impose thoughts and feelings upon those who read them. And he has to be great; he must have a quality of soul that is profound and, because it is profound, is universal. His soul plunges deeper and soars higher than the fashionable feelings of his day. Conventions of sensibility may fade away, and others come to take their place, but the rhythm of his deep waves is undisturbed by these superficial rufflings. He is a prophet of what is eternal in the human soul.

There is always, at all times and in all places, a shallow literature of convention and fashion, created by superficial sensibilities, for the amusement of those many people who require from an author a reflection of their idle selves and satisfaction of their trivial appetites. They turn away in fear from the prospect of being made to see unfamiliar sights, to feel disturbing feelings, or to think thoughts beyond the reaches of their souls, which are hide-bound for lack of exercise. They have a vague presentiment how uncomfortable, how positively catastrophic, it would be if their souls were to be wakened into life, and they avoid the danger as they would the plague – but still more instinctively. A dead soul is bound to shrink from contact with a live one. They want their literature soothing and narcotic and innocuous. 'How beautiful,' they murmur at their tea-parties, 'and what style!' Yet a glimpse of true beauty would frighten them out of their lives, and an inkling of the real nature of style would send their timorous minds squealing down the road to perdition.

For there is something awful and terrible in the work of a great writer, even though he may be, like Dickens or Gogol, a master of what is called Comedy, for the Comedy that does not consist in the bandying of airy repartee is based on a savage and ruthless vision into the nakedness of human nature. The comedist laughs, we all laugh; but if we were to stop laughing, something queer might happen. We have to keep Sairey Gamp under control, lest she become a portent, and Tartufe lest he become a monster. Even Falstaff may develop a trick of growing uncomfortably titanic. And the nearer we approach to the living soul of the great writer, the more are we aware of the immensities between which that life of his is perilously swung. For as we approach the creative centre of his work, we are able to read it, we directly experience it, as the record of a struggle for being. His books are the battle-ground of his soul. In them he fights for life and a faith without which life cannot exist, and his struggle is the more terrible, the more moving, and the more profound, because he is by nature aware of so much more than other men. His faith must justify more, just as his life must include more, than the faiths and lives of other men.

And just because the great writer is an adventurer on behalf of humanity and is, in these latter days at least, the archetype of conscious man, his effort is essentially religious; but essentially, not superficially. We shall not discover much about the bond between literature and religion by hunting through the great writers for sentences that may be used for texts for sermons. The writer is seldom occupied in praising God; his effort is to discover or to rediscover Him. An anthology of snippets like —

'A robin redbreast in a cage
Puts all Heaven in a rage'

may be edifying and reassuring as tending to show that these lawless and incalculable persons are really pillars of orthodoxy. But the fact remains that they are nothing of the kind. They search for God because they are pre-eminently men, and because it is a law of the living human soul that the connection must somehow be established. But theirs are perilous adventures, and they do not return from them to the calm safety of a harbour they have left. If they find a harbour, it is a new one, not by any means to be identified with the old. They are not prodigal sons who return, having wasted their substance, to their father; far rather, in their rediscovery of God, do they recreate the reality of religion. Their progress ends not in an abjuration of their error, but in a triumph of their truth.

But this assumption that literature is the record of a soul's struggle after life and God may not appear so necessary and self-evident to my readers as it does to me. 'Think of *Tom Jones*,' they may say, 'or *Pride and Prejudice* or *Alice in Wonderland* – where is the soul-struggle in them?' Well, honestly, I do not believe it is there. There is a soul manifest in Fielding's and Jane Austen's books, otherwise they would not have the strong individuality we recognize in them; but it is not a struggling soul. Nevertheless, if we look at the whole course of Western literature since the Renaissance, we shall find that placid and undisturbed personalities like these are not really characteristic. The great figures of the period are shaped after the pattern of Shakespeare – they are nearly all what is generally called 'Romantics.' But if we regard Romanticism as an attitude of soul which was unknown before it descended upon Europe in the person of Jean-Jacques Rousseau, or if we think of it parochially as a return to nature and a revolt against convention on the part of a handful of English poets at the beginning of the nineteenth century, we shall never understand either Romanticism or the epoch of consciousness in which we live. Romanticism was something that happened to the European soul after the Renaissance; and the essential fact of the Renaissance was that man asserted his independence of an external spiritual authority. It was a movement of expansion and growth, which became vaguely conscious of itself because of the New Learning. Men, who had long been silently chafing against the restraints of an established and omnipotent religion which by the mere magnitude of its organization had lost contact with the individual soul, gained confidence in their own impulses from the sudden revelation of an epoch before their own. They saw that a time had been when the spirit of free inquiry had flourished, and men like themselves had lived outside the shadow of the terror of death and the life to come. The veil of mist that had obscured the past from them and made them feel that the dispensation under which they lived was established in the very nature of the universe was suddenly rolled away. They could see what had been; therefore they could see that what was was not absolute, but relative, not the eternal creation of God, but the temporal handiwork of man.

To gain some inkling of what the Renaissance meant, one has only to remember the lovely and famous lyric of Villon, the enchanting and lonely cry of the bewildered human spirit in the Dark Ages:

> 'Dites moi ou nen quel pays
> Est Flora la belle Romaine
> Archipiada ni Thais
> Qui fust sa cousine germaine?'

For the answer to that question is that 'Flora, the lovely Roman,' and Archipiada never were. Only one name of the three has come unscathed through the darkness of ignorance; the other two are fragmentary echoes of a forgotten past. There was nothing for Villon but the present, and the shadow of the Church and the Church's damnation over all. No doubt the sun shone then, and the trees burst into bud in the spring, and the corn ripened in the fields, and women were fair, and man's senses free to enjoy them; but the ambit of the human soul was circumscribed. It glanced backward into a darkness and forward into a terror. It was afraid.

The Renaissance meant for a moment the end of

fear. The individual could stand alone once more, after more than a thousand years. And one of the first-fruits of his standing alone was the discovery that he was alone indeed. Galileo built his telescope and found that the earth moved round the sun. That was the great symbolic discovery of the Renaissance. And Shakespeare's work is the reaction of a prophetic soul to the discovery. It does not matter in the least whether Shakespeare knew of it or not; for Galileo's discovery was only the outward, visible sign of an inward and spiritual event, an event which we can see working in Shakespeare's soul. Man was not the centre of the universe, and man stood alone to face his destiny. The burden of the modern consciousness had begun.

Now, the foundation of the modern consciousness is this, that the individual man takes his stand apart and alone, without the support of any authority, and claims to pass judgment for himself upon the life of which he is a part. He asks: By what, for what, shall he live? Here he is, involved in a vast process, in which evil seems as paramount as good, in which the noblest courage and the basest cowardice find a common end in death; here he is, caught into a senseless and unmeaning riot in which glimpses of truth and beauty are apparently vouchsafed solely in order that man should be aware of the falsehood and ugliness which triumph over them. And he rebels against the

173

sum of things. The modern consciousness is primarily a consciousness of rebellion; it begins with the demand that life should satisfy the individual's sense of justice and harmony.

And the old answer of orthodox Christianity, that the injustice and the pain of this life would be redeemed in a life to come, could satisfy no more. Men had come to feel that this life was a certainty and the future life a surmise which they had suffered to grow into a terror, frightening them from their true fulfilment on earth. The modern consciousness begins historically with the repudiation of organised Christianity; it begins with the moment when men found in themselves the courage to doubt the life to come, and to free themselves from its menace in order to live this life more fully. It was necessary that man should come to his full stature, and that could only be done, as always, by his standing alone and assuming full responsibility for himself. What he *knew* to be true, that alone was true.

'What I know to be true, that alone is true.' This has been the blazon on the banner of the Western consciousness since the Renaissance. It seems a simple statement, just a straightforward challenge to external spiritual authority. And yet, in fact, that simple statement includes within it all the potentialities of the human soul. The whole of the human mystery is contained in the words 'I know,' just as it

174

is contained in the words 'I am.' For what am I? and what is it that I know? The various answers to those ultimate questions mark the phases of the modern consciousness. But these phases are spiritual and transcendental; they are not neatly chronological. Though we can say truly that from the Renaissance to the present day the large and general movement has been towards seeking an ever-deeper answer, it is equally true to say and equally important to recognize that there have been minds prophetic of the future. Not until Keats does a mind of the same order, not until Tolstoi and Dostoevsky does a mind of the same scope and comprehensiveness, as Shakespeare's arise in European literature, and we find them following out the path marked out for them in Shakespeare's drama. Shakespeare had forefelt and foreknown their destiny; he had passed through the same discomfiture and arrived at the same necessity. All the literature which falls between those Titans of the modern consciousness is but a partial rediscovery of what Shakespeare already knew.

There have been, there are eternally, two great types of answer to the question 'What do I know?' There is the answer, 'I know the external world,' and there is the answer 'I know myself.' At any moment in human history one or other of them is usually preponderant. For they correspond to two different *kinds* of knowledge. The knowledge of the external world is a knowledge wherein the laws of cause and effect are operant; it is a rational knowledge of a realm of necessity, wherein the total conditions at a given moment are totally determined by the total conditions at the moment immediately before. There is no room for freedom in this world, and, in fact, no freedom is recognized. The knowledge of myself, on the other hand, or, as we may call it for the sake of symmetry, the knowledge of the internal world, is a knowledge which is not governed by laws of cause and effect; it is an irrational, immediate knowledge, of a realm of freedom wherein the total conditions at a given moment are never totally determined by the total conditions at the moment before. There is no room for necessity in this world, and in fact no necessity is recognized.

Both these kinds of knowledge are knowledge. It is as impossible for me to deny that two and two make four as it is for me to deny that I am free. But these kinds of knowledge are utterly different: one seems to come to me from without, the other to surge upward from within. And they are irreconcilable. The one, in pursuit of its own completeness, demands that the internal world should be of the same substance and subject to the same laws as the external world, that my integral and inviolable soul should be part of the realm of necessity, which seems absurd. The other, in pursuit of its completeness, demands that I should know the external world immediately as I know myself, which seems impossible.

This is the great paradox of the modern consciousness. It is, of course, much older than the Renaissance. It is universal in the world, and eternal in the human mind. But the awareness of the paradox has become most acute and reached an extreme of anxiety and indecision in the centuries since the Renaissance. For more than three hundred years – ever since the organized Christian Church ceased to be an unquestioned authority for the most gifted human minds – men have agonized over this paradox. The world has gone on; there have been famine and prosperity, and happiness and suffering, and wealth and poverty, just as there have always been. There have been colossal progress and colossal war, until now deep in our irrational souls we feel that we have reached a climacteric. The signs and tokens of madness and catastrophe multiply; and we begin to surmise that the paradox of the modern consciousness may be on the point of some slow solution.

But that is beyond my present scope. What is to be insisted upon here is, first, that the paradox is a religious problem – to be more accurate still, it is *the* religious problem, the only religious problem – and, secondly, that modern literature from the Renaissance until to-day has been pre-eminently occupied with it.

Now, it is clear, from the very nature of the paradox, that no intellectual resolution is conceivable. The primary fact is man's consciousness of his own existence, his knowledge of himself as free: and that is an irrational knowledge. Whatever man does he must not deny this, simply because he will be forced to deny his own denial. He cannot really mechanize himself; if he attempts to, he merely deceives himself. The attempt to find a resolution from the side of the external world, *sub specie necessitatis*, is doomed to failure. So the resolution must be sought from the side of the internal world, *sub specie libertatis*. In other words man, is inevitably driven to seek a non-rational comprehension of the world. He cannot help himself: he must find a harmony: he cannot *live* in rebellion: he must reintegrate himself into life. So we find him cleaving, in literature, to the evidence of those moments of profound apprehension —

> 'When all the burden and the mystery
> Is lightened and . . .
> We see into the life of things.'

The validity of such moments of apprehension is for the apprehender unquestioned: the quality of vision, to him who experiences it, is indubitable. For that moment he knows the world, even as he knows himself.

We may, if we like, call this moment of apprehen-

sion mystical. The name does not matter. Those
who feel they can dismiss a knowledge when they
have labelled it 'mystical' may be freely permitted to
smile their dismissal. It does not matter, indeed,
whether we call it mystical, provided only that if we
do, we remember that our immediate knowledge of
our own self-existence is not a whit less 'mystical'
than this. These perceptions are of the same order;
and it may even be that in the last analysis one is not
more intermittent than the other. The point of
present importance, however, is that this 'mystical'
resolution of the paradox is what really distinguishes
'the Romantic movement' in modern literature. On
this Rousseau staked his all: this was at the creative
centre of Wordsworth, of Shelley, of Keats, and of
Coleridge. The truest and deepest knowledge they
found in themselves was in a moment of immediate
apprehension of the unity of the world. They saw,
or felt that they saw, that the great external world was
not subject to the law of necessity – or rather not to
the rational law of necessity: it was a living thing, an
organism, which they knew as they knew the life
within them. And it may seem strange that their
apprehension of it should have been, in some sort,
also an apprehension of necessity: of the necessity
that what they saw must be thus and not otherwise.
But this will seem strange only because we are hypno-
tized by words, and find it hard to realize that there

is not one necessity, but two necessities, just as there is not one knowledge, but two knowledges. There is the necessity of the inanimate world conceived by the intellect, which is the necessary dependence of effect upon cause: and there is the necessity of the living organism, apprehended immediately, a compulsion to follow its own inward law of life. The 'mystical' vision is a vision of *organic* necessity.

Such is the resolution of the great paradox sought by what is called the Romantic movement. It needs no saying that it is a deeply religious answer to a deeply religious problem. In any one of the true Romantics you may find at any moment a formulation of this perception of organic necessity as a perception of God: and I for my own part am convinced that if it is not a vision of God, it is assuredly a premonition of the divine. Here, for instance, is Robert Burns's statement.

'We know nothing, or next to nothing, of the structure of our souls, so we cannot account for those seeming caprices in them, that one should be particularly pleased with this thing, or struck with that, which, on minds of a different cast, makes no extraordinary impression. I have some favourite flowers in spring, among which are the mountain-daisy, the harebell, the foxglove, the wild-brier rose, the budding birch, and the hoary hawthorn, that I view and hang over with particular delight. I never hear the loud, solitary whistle of the curlew in a summer noon, or the wild mixing cadence of a troop of grey plover in an autumnal morning, without feeling an elevation of soul like the enthusiasm of devotion or poetry. Tell me, my dear friend, to what can this be owing? Are we a piece of machinery, which, like the Æolian harp, passive, takes the impression of the passing accident; or do these wordings argue something within us above the trodden clod? I own myself partial to such proofs of those awful and important realities: a God that made all things, man's immaterial and immortal nature, and a world of weal or woe beyond the grave.'

I choose that from Burns rather than a more famous passage from Keats because it is so easily and so often assumed that the marvellous singer was really 'the ignorant ploughboy' of legend and outside the charmed circle of our Romantic poets. He was of them, equal among equals.

But the peril of such perceptions is that they are momentary: they do not endure. Man may build a belief upon moments; yet he cannot live by them. The greater Romantics knew this also. Not a single one of those whom our literary history is accustomed to call our Romantics — except the Keats of the revised *Hyperion* — belonged to this higher order.

And we shall never understand the real nature or the deep significance of Romanticism until we understand that the whole of the epoch which we have called the modern consciousness is Romantic. The brief period which usually goes by that name is only a little segment of a great curve – a Romanticism within a Romanticism, as it were. Romanticism, essentially, is a movement of the soul which begins with the assertion of the I AM against all external spiritual authority, which proceeds from this condition of rebellion and isolation to a new life-adjustment, and goes on towards the ultimate recognition of a new principle of authority in and through the deeper knowledge of the self. Briefly, it may be called the rediscovery of the greater I AM through the lesser I AM. The phases of this great rhythmical motion are marked in the history of the human spirit from the Renaissance till to-day; but, as I have said, they are not wholly chronological. There were prophetic souls. At the beginning of the epoch stands Shakespeare, who comprehends within himself – 'the prophetic soul of the wide world, dreaming on things to come' – the whole movement of which lesser men were to manifest the phases after him. Shakespeare is a greater Romantic; so were Tolstoi and Dostoevsky; so was, in the essential at least, Walt Whitman.

The distinctive quality of those whom I call the

greater Romantics is that they should have completed within themselves the cycle of their being: in them the wheel has turned full circle. They have their moments of comprehension — one has only to read *The Phœnix and Turtle* to know how profound was the momentary understanding and acquiescence of Shakespeare — but the moment does not endure. Not that it ever loses its validity or its meaning; it remains as an earnest of the comprehension that may be, as a premonition of the harmony that is. But it is not enough; it is one-sided; implicit within it is a denial of life. Man cannot live by groping backward after old ecstasies. His knowledge must be steady and unwavering. It must not be intermittent; it must not be suprasensual; it must be a possession for ever. That is the crucial point. Man must *possess* his knowledge. It must not come to him as a visitant, and when it leaves him, leave him naked to the winds of reality. It is not a final, perhaps not even a human victory, that he should triumph for a moment over the world of necessity and sink back to live in it as an alien and a sojourner. The reconciliation between the kingdom of necessity and the kingdom of freedom must not be subject to such vicissitude. In the last resort, it cannot be one-sided: or it will fail.

What distinguishes the greater Romantics is the recognition of the need of a solution of the paradox that is not one-sided. It is that humanity must find rest, not in a fleeting moment of heightened consciousness, but in a change of consciousness itself. A new beginning will be made, and a new generation born for which the paradox will not exist. The secular division between the intellectual consciousness (of necessity) and the intuitional consciousness (of freedom) will be no more. There will be a *known* harmony between the mysterious and as yet undiscovered reality which lies beneath the world of material phenomena and the reality of ourselves.

It is useless to try to describe this condition. A change, a fundamental change, in the human consciousness can only be dimly imagined and only symbolically expressed. Shakespeare's symbols are plain to read for those who can read symbols at all. There was a moment when all that he had done had no more interest for him; when the writing of even the mightiest tragedies was for him a thing of no concern. The works of his latest period, which no one knows whether to call tragedies or comedies, works which are truly neither and for the most part are not in any intelligible sense works of art at all, have this meaning written plainly upon them. 'I am weary, weary; I am interested in one thing alone – to imagine the birth of a new generation for whom my struggles and torments and victories shall be only a dim, ancestral memory. The rest is for me only the idle weaving of words.' And so, after playing half-

184

wistfully with the figures of his imagination, in *The Winter's Tale*, in *Cymbeline*, in that part of *Pericles* that is indisputably his, after creating Perdita and Imogen and Marina, he gathered his strength together and conquered his own weariness to prophesy in *The Tempest*. The old consciousness fades away in Prospero; the greatest of all its inheritors resigns it to make way for the coming of a new consciousness in his loved child Miranda —

'O brave new world that has such people in it!'

I believe that *The Tempest* is the most perfect prophetic achievement of the Western mind. It is not Shakespeare's greatest work of art; in one deep sense it is not a work of art at all, for the prime condition of its creation was that art in the ordinary meaning should have been relinquished and rejected. It is — if we are to call it art at all — the art that arises out of Shakespeare's deliberate abandonment of art. It belongs to the order of Tolstoi's later parables; but it it still more profound than they are. It stands on the very verge of a condition that still lies far before the human soul. In Shakespeare the wheel had truly turned full circle, and because he was the prophet of what was to come, his last word is still the latest.

No Western mind has passed beyond *The Tempest*; none has gone so far.

'Shakespeare (says Novalis) was no calculator, no

learned thinker; he was a mighty, many-gifted soul, whose feelings and works, like products of nature, bear the stamp of the same spirit; and in which the best and deepest of observers will still find new harmonies with the infinite structure of the universe; concurrences with later ideas, affinities with the higher powers and senses of man. They are emblematic, have many meanings, are simple and inexhaustible, like products of nature; and nothing more unsuitable could be said of them than they are works of art, in that narrow mechanical acceptation of the word.'

We are bound ever again and finally to return to Shakespeare in our pursuit of an understanding of the whole spiritual history of man since the Renaissance. Up to Shakespeare the spiritual history of man — I speak of the West alone — is comprehended within the Church; with him, it passes outside the Church. The severance was necessary and inevitable, for the sake of religion itself; simply because religion, if it is to be more than a comfortable and convenient narcotic, must be based on a challenge of the nature of things by the free spirit of man. And that again simply because man cannot *accept* certainties; he must discover them. An accepted certainty is not a certainty, a discovered certainty is. It is futile therefore for the priest to point to the final condition of a Shakespeare, a Tolstoi, or a Dostoevsky, and say that he knew it all before. Is it not written in the Gospel: 'Except ye be born again, ye shall in no wise enter into the Kingdom of Heaven'? There, indeed, it is written. But how many people know what it means as these champions of humanity knew? No matter how finally, how beautifully, how profoundly Christ formulated the everlasting truths of religion, in order to know that they are everlasting, in order to know quite simply what they mean, man must rediscover them in himself.

The deepest-flowing tradition of Western literature is the process of challenge by the free human spirit ending in that rediscovery. If we can see that it is inevitable, it is only in so far as we can see that religion is a necessary motion of the human soul, a fundamental rhythm of man's being. Then it is plain that it must be fulfilled in literature which is primarily an expression of that being. Then we can also recognize that there are greater and smaller fulfilments. In the greater spirits the wheel truly turns full circle; in the lesser, it turns only half or quarter of the way. And, further, among these incomplete revolutions some may be conscious and others only instinctive. In those whom I have called the lesser Romantics – from Rousseau to Amiel – the fulfilments are conscious. The moment of vision and understanding is deliberately sought and directly acknowledged by these writers themselves, and it has been recognized by all men of religion who are not mere dogmatists as a central moment of religious experience. But we may go farther than this, and declare that the originating experience of any truly creative work of literature, however small, is in some measure, and perhaps essentially, religious. That recognition by the writer of his theme, that delighted apprehension of his material, in the world outside him or within, seems to be nothing else than the sudden perception that an immaterial and all-pervading essence can be contained in a single symbol. What is perceived is perceived as something much greater than it is: as the philosophers put it, the universal is apprehended in and through the particular. This profound emotional recognition of the particular object or happening, as significant, as typical, as characteristic – an act of recognition which lies at the basis of all literary art and is as necessary to the simplest poem as it is recurrent in every considerable work of literature – seems to me fundamentally religious. There is a communication between mystery and mystery, between the unknown soul and the unknown reality; at one particular point in the texture of life the hidden truth seems to break through the veil.

'Dans certains états de l'âme presque surnaturels

(wrote Baudelaire) la profondeur de la vie se revèle tout entière dans le spectacle, si ordinaire qu'il soit, qu'on a sous les yeux: il en devient le symbole.'

Even this *âme damnée* had to admit in his honesty that the states of soul were 'almost supernatural'; and these supernatural states, which may be infinitesimal or overwhelming, these perceptions of a universal significance in the particular, are the primary stuff out of which literature is created.[1]

We have thus been working, as it were backwards, through a problem so vast and evasive that it might well be thought that a more orderly and logical presentment was indispensable. But, in sober truth, the subject is too vast for such a treatment in an essay. I have aimed at emphasizing those elements in it which seem to me to be even now but inadequately recognized. It is not worth while, in this place and with these necessary limitations, to insist upon a truth that is at the present time fairly generally, if half-heartedly, admitted: namely, that there is an intimate connection between both the creative perceptions that animate a work of literature and the responses those perceptions awaken in us, and the religious experience. But what seem to me the larger truths are not generally accepted. These, as I see them, are:

[1] For a more detailed exposition of this argument, the reader may be referred to the writer's *The Problem of Style*.

First, that religion is the deepest and most necessary motion of the free human soul; as it were, a reflection in the consciousness of the inevitable adjustment to the primary law of life; and that it follows that literature, which is the most complete expression of the free human soul, *must* be religious, and that the greater the literature is, the more religious must it be. This seems to me axiomatic: to one who has apprehended the full content of the word 'religion' not even arguable. It can be recognized or not recognized: that is all.

Secondly, that religion, being of this fundamental kind, is by nature not to be confined in one medium of expression. At one time it may be an organized Church which is the preponderant vehicle of the religious tradition. The continual process of rediscovery in the free human soul of the truth of religion may be accomplished at certain times mainly within a Church, at others mainly without it. This will depend on whether the measure of freedom attainable by the soul is greater within a Church than without, or greater without than within, at any given time. Where the freedom is greater, there will the stream of the vital religious tradition inevitably flow, because complete freedom is the necessary pre-condition of the religious rediscovery. Only through the fullest exploration of life can man *know* the laws of life.

Thirdly, the historical proposition that with the Renaissance the stream of religious tradition began to flow mainly outside the Church. Science took upon itself the fulfilment of the outward exploration, literature the fulfilment of the inward exploration of life; and literature, whose course was indicated in the prophetic mind of Shakespeare, assumed, sometimes consciously, sometimes unconsciously, the task of finding a mode of reconciliation between the realm of necessity and the realm of freedom. For the law of religious rediscovery is that man must apprehend the universe of his fullest knowledge, within and without, as an *organic* unity.

Fourthly, that the conclusion reached by the literature which is most deeply expressive of the modern consciousness is that a fundamental change or rebirth of the human consciousness is necessary. Whether it is inevitable is another matter, outside the scope of this essay: I believe that it is.

Fifthly, that the whole great movement of the modern consciousness can be expressed completely for those who have experienced it within themselves, but only for those, in the sayings of Christ. As Shakespeare is prophetic of the last, modern era of the Western consciousness, Christ was prophetic of the whole epoch, of which this last modern era is the culminating part.

Finally, that literature is become the great religious

adventure of the human soul, simply because it affords the only complete expression to the adventuring human soul, and the human soul is bound upon an adventure which is necessarily religious. The meeting-ground of the lesser I AM with the greater I AM is still, after all the centuries, almost an unknown territory. *Hic Rhodus, hic salta.*

Religion and Christianity

OF LATE I HAVE BEEN BROUGHT IN-
to contact with many members of the Christian
Church — Roman Catholics and Anglicans. It is not
easy to say why it should have happened so. Possibly
it is because I have become curious about these
things and eager to discover for myself what reality
there is in Christianity to-day; so that I have paused
to ask and listen where in the old days I would have
passed by on the other side. Or it may be — and this
is nearer to my own belief — that there is some sort of
destiny and design in these encounters; for it seems
to me that a moment may come in one's life whence-
forward 'everything has a meaning' and circumstances put off for ever their old appearance of for-
tuitousness.

There were many things I desired to learn; but the
chief of all was this. I wanted to learn *how* it was
possible for a man to believe in what I call the dogmas of Christianity, whether at their simplest in the
Apostles' Creed of the English Church or at their
most complicated in the (to me scarcely intelligible)
doctrines of the Roman Catholic. The attitude of
mind and soul which such a belief seemed to demand
was so alien to my own that I longed to know whether
it really existed. For I think I know from my own
experience what belief actually is; I believe that there

is a God and that I have a soul. It has taken me many years and much painful experience to reach a knowledge of those truths: I knew them both at the same moment, and I believe I know that knowledge of the one depends upon knowledge of the other. You cannot believe you have a soul, you cannot believe in your own real and independent existence, without believing in the existence of God. And this belief is just as simple and certain as the knowledge that I am sitting now in a ridiculously small armchair before a gas-fire, writing with an old draughtboard on my knees for a desk. I would, as I have said before, rather call this knowledge than belief; but the name is of no great consequence.

Now it seemed to me, and seems no less to-day, that it is inconceivable and unimaginable that any human being should believe in the dogmas of the Christian Church in the same way that I believe in the existence of God and of my own soul. The things to be believed are of a totally different order, and the luminous certainty with which it is possible to apprehend the interdependent existence of God and one's self is quite inconceivable with regard to the formulated creeds of the Christian Church. Moreover, it seemed, and still seems, plain to me that if a man knew the former, he must inevitably see that the latter were irrelevant.

My curiosity became active some three months ago

when chance threw me together with an eminent
Roman Catholic, and in the course of a vaguely theological conversation, I spontaneously confessed my
utter inability to understand *how* a Roman Catholic
believed what he was supposed to believe. Did he
possess (I wondered) some whole faculty of soul
which had been denied to me? For at that time,
though it seemed to me scarcely credible, I was willing to admit such a possibility. My astonishment
was profound and overwhelming when I heard my
companion reply: 'Oh, all that's very easy, you know,
if you can manage to believe in the existence of God:
that's where the real difficulty comes in.' And I
understood immediately from the way he spoke that
it was a very real difficulty for him, and moreover
that he had not solved it.

Perhaps that reply will not appear so extraordinary
to my readers as it appeared to me. But it struck me
as an astonishing confession, the more astonishing
because he evidently felt that there was nothing very
astonishing in it. For a moment I was dumb. Then
I said: 'But I *know* that God exists.' There followed
a much longer silence; it was strange and oppressive.
'You're lucky,' he said at last. But during the
silence my mind had been busy, with some such
train of thought as this: 'He finds it easy to believe in
dogma, and hard to believe in God: I find it inevitable to believe in the existence of God, and impos-

sible for that very reason to believe in dogma. And somehow his confession confirms my own surmise: that it is impossible to reconcile a belief in dogma with a self-discovered certainty of the existence of God. He finds it easy to accept the dogmas, *if* he can believe that God exists, because his belief is in the main an intellectual act. He manages, by some sleight of brain, to *conceive* for a moment the existence of a God; and this intellectually conceived God of his has intellectually conceived attributes — omnipotence, omniscience, and the rest. Therefore, why should he not work miracles? Why not, indeed? But the fact remains that a God whom you have to conceive intellectually is a God of whose existence you are not, never have been, and never will be certain. For a God of whom you are certain must reject as alien, attributes derived from a faculty of the soul which is but a fragment or a facet of the consciousness that knows him.'

So I mused within myself; and settled the problem *how* a man believes in Christian dogma, settled the problem, that is, to my own satisfaction. He does not believe, as I understand belief. Instead he achieves some sort of willing suspension of disbelief. I know that condition also from my own experience; and I also know that the two conditions are as different from each other as twilight is different from the brightness of a noonday sun.

196

Nevertheless, I wanted to learn more. I met more professing Christians of many kinds; and almost always, in one form or another, the answer was the same. They had not belief, not the irrefragable and luminous certainty of the existence of God, which alone to me deserves the name of belief in God, but some willing or anxious suspension of disbelief, which cannot take its place. And I began to wonder why they should be willing or anxious to conjure thus with themselves, for to me such efforts seem a derogation from human dignity. It lies in the very dignity of man to stand or fall by his own knowledge. His duties to himself in this regard are two: first, not to shut himself off from knowledge by any preconceived idea that knowledge can be only of one single and familiar kind, but to keep himself open to the entrance of certainty whencesoever it may come — and a certainty is quite simply defined: it is a conviction by which a man is prepared to live and, if need be, to die — and the second duty of a man is this: not to suffer himself to go an inch beyond his own knowledge, for beyond those bounds the realms of confusion and disquiet begin.

To one who holds this as the strongest of all his convictions, it was naturally a matter for wonder that there should be so many men who were willing to disobey this prime law of humanity. How could they do such a thing? What was their motive, and what their reward? And to this, as I talked to them, an answer slowly became manifest. Again it surprised me, surprised me first by its simplicity, and then by my own failure to have guessed at it. For their motive is fear, and their reward a refuge from the isolation which they fear. The prospect of being alone, to stand or fall by their own knowledge is intolerable to them. For this cause men have formed a society which is the Christian Church; for this cause they have devised declarations of membership which are the dogmas and creeds I find it so impossible to accept or to understand or even to value. And these declarations of membership are indeed irrelevant, for they are designed for a general acceptance, and are therefore intellectual formulations of that which cannot be formulated intellectually without being perverted and destroyed.

The truth of the matter, as I pondered over it, appeared to me thus: that the man who believes in God does not need a Church. He does not need the support of an organized community because he has learned to stand alone; and it is inevitable that he should have learned to stand alone, because only by complete isolation can a man come to the certainty of the existence of God and of himself. And this thought of mine quickly became simplified into this clear opinion: that humanity is divided into men who are willing to stand alone and those who are not, and, further, that the God of those who will stand alone is different from the God of those who will not. The one God does not need to be defined because He does not need to be shared; in order to believe in Him the man who stands alone does not need that others should partake of his own belief. He would like them to reach it, he would do all that lies in him to hasten that day; but he cannot do much, for he knows that each must reach it by his own way: and that way also must be a way of isolation.

Perhaps this great division is not so crystal-clear to others as it is to me. I think it a very important division, and one which, if we follow it, takes us direct to the heart of the age-old problem: What *is* Christianity? We find that the answer is that Christianity is two distinct and different things.

For the man who is willing to stand alone, it is clear beyond all question that the God of Jesus Christ is the God of a man who stood alone. There is no difficulty. The meaning of the most mysterious words of Jesus Christ can be rediscovered and ratified within himself by any man who will have the courage of his isolation, and he will know that Christ was indeed the great pioneer and champion of humanity in the epoch in which we live. He explored life on our behalf, and he made clear the road by which any man who has the courage can make the crucial discovery of God's existence and his own. And the very condition of that exploration and discovery was that Christ should be a man: for it is not by any historical arguments that the man who stands alone denies the divinity of Christ. Moreover, he does not deny anything to Christ; he is making a claim on his behalf; he claims the complete humanity of Christ, because it is necessary to the complete significance of Christ, because only thus can he be truly understood, or truly loved, or truly followed. For to follow Christ is not to take simple words of his and try to obey them. You cannot know what they mean until you have followed him in a deeper sense than this. When he said: 'My little children, love one another,' he meant another kind of love than that which the kind-hearted lavish upon their friends. And the only way to know what it means is to have followed him into utter isolation, to have had one's forty days in the wilderness, to have fought down in oneself the terrible temptation to turn stones into bread, to have refused to the very last spark of one's strength to cheat oneself — 'This once I will endure to the end, though I die' — to have believed in nothing, to have become nothing, and to be born again. Then one begins to know something about God and oneself and love, that can be learned from no man and no Church.

Now this is not easy; it is painful. Above all, it is intensely individualistic, though the final result is quite the reverse of individualistic. But human beings who are lonely and afraid will not take the plunge into their own loneliness; they crave for some nearer and more comfortable way. After all, they feel, they can't be expected to do such things: they were not made to stand alone. And quite early they took precautions against such efforts being required of them by declaring that Christ was not human, but divine. That may sound cynical; I have no wish to be cynical: but the fact is that the Christ who is man demands infinitely more from men than the Christ who is God. The loyalty required is of an altogether more exacting kind, simply because it is a loyalty between men as men, and one which must be obeyed and pursued alone. Which is precisely what human beings, as a whole, most wish to avoid. They do not want to act for themselves, or to take responsibility for themselves. Therefore, the intense individualism of Christ was changed, by the single stroke of deifying him, into an excuse for its opposite: he became the God of a Church, instead of the example of a man.

I am not suggesting (as Dostoevsky suggested in *The Grand Inquisitor*) that the change was deliberate and Machiavellian. It is simply explained by the fact that men are afraid of standing alone, and because they are afraid, they cannot understand the man who does. Christ appeared superhuman to his disciples. Doubtless, they loved him; but that they understood

him no one who reads the Gospel narratives can believe for a moment. They were simple Jews who believed he was the Messiah who should restore Israel.
When he spoke of the Kingdom of Heaven, they
believed he was speaking of the Jewish kingdom;
when he said 'the Kingdom of Heaven is within you,'
his words seemed to them unintelligible and mysterious. Quite naturally they felt that he was a man of
higher order than themselves, and they made him a
God: there was nothing else for them to do. And
slowly and inevitably a great Church was organized
to cover the Western world – the Christian Church.
And look at the Western World to-day!

Christianity has failed, but not Christ. He has not
been tried, save by lonely individuals whose words
are remembered through the ages as his are remembered. There is nothing mysterious about his gospel
and his example; it is simply this: Take responsibility for yourself and stand alone. But there are
many mysteries to be discovered if you take that road.
And I believe that the future depends upon those who
will take it, and on them alone. For surely we have
learned that there is nothing to hope for from justice,
or organization, or progress, or common sense, or any
of the hundred fetishes on which men pin their faith.
'Improve the mechanics of civilization!' cries one;
'Follow the dictates of mere rational expediency!'
cries another; and all will, in spite of all, be well.

Nonsense! No one believes it, least of all those who cry out. And Lord Birkenhead's cynicisms evoke a reply as feeble as they themselves are cheap. 'Why don't the Churches act?' comes yet another plaintive bleat. As though a Church ever did or ever could *act* save as a nation or an army! Why not say: 'Please be good, everybody!' and have done with it?

But indeed the time is long past when we could delude ourselves into depending upon things which other men must do with us, if they are to be done at all. Can we even yet not realize that there is no hope in other men, and that there is, above all, no hope in the man who builds his hope on other men? There is hope in the man who will be and will do, alone. For the salvation of the world depends upon individuals, upon men who are willing to pay the debt they owe to their dignity as human beings by fighting out the battle in themselves until they possess their souls. They will understand one another; they will know each other at a glance or at a word; they will not need societies, or organizations, or churches in order to be strong. Humanity has sought strength in masses too long and too disastrously. Let it try the way of separation; then it may achieve the unknown unity which it dumbly craves.

(November, 1924.)

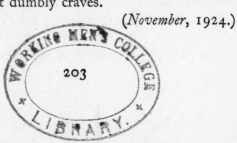

203

Heads or Tails?

THERE ARE TWO WORLDS. NOT THIS one and the next. I know nothing about the next, anyhow. But two worlds here and now. Two co-existent worlds that perplex me.

They perplex me — it would be truer to say — chiefly when I think about them; and I think about them chiefly when I am suddenly compelled to. Then I cannot reconcile them. It seems to me that I was born subject to both, and that I am troubled by a divided allegiance.

If I were consistent, I should call them 'the world within' and 'the world without.' But that is too solemn. O Lord, deliver me from my besetting virtue, which is solemnity! Things are much more truly seen, if we can look at them with a twinkle in the eye. I am afraid mine do not twinkle quite so readily as they ought. Give me the smallest chance, the merest fraction of a second to wind myself up, and I am tense, at strain, with the air of one who is taking a decision for all eternity.

It is not that I really feel things in that way. Once upon a time I used to; but that has changed. (*Umberufen!*) What remains, however, is some old trick of the mechanism, so that if I have to point out to the greengrocer that he is charging me twopence too much on a dozen oranges, I lapse immediately into the attitude of Achilles defying the lightning. All for twopence! And I still seem to spend on catching a train, or on looking for a bed in an unfamiliar town, energy enough to supply the whole of England with electric light for a day.

So I have to take precautions against my mechanism, which from two words or two ideas, always pushes the more portentous to the tip of my tongue. I will not talk of 'the world within' and 'the world without' any more just now. It is Christmas time. Moreover, I have been to the play – *Our Betters*, by Somerset Maugham. It is not a very good play. Mr. Maugham suffered also from the divided soul: he couldn't make up his mind between satire and sentiment. But he makes somebody say: 'If we all thought about things the night before the same as we do the morning after,' life would be a much simpler affair than it is.

Much simpler, no doubt; but very different from what it is. If it had been so, indeed, in *Our Betters*, Mr. Maugham would have been left without a play at all. But the division suits me better than the more solemn one that is habitual.

These then are the two worlds: the world of the night before and the world of the morning after. Everybody has a foot, if not a foothold, in both of them. Some people, most people perhaps, are pretty solidly planted in one of them, and towards the other they behave like little babies who go to the seaside for the first time in their lives. The rounded froth of a spent wave slides swiftly up the sand; it touches the tip of their toes, and they scuttle shrieking back to their element. Contrariwise, I suppose the little fishes, when they are caught up beyond the high surf barrier, bundled into the no-man's-land of the broken waves, and touch the terrifying shingle, give an agonized flick with their fins and shoot into the deep once more.

I am neither a little child nor a little fish. I am a merman (if I am kind to myself) or a monster (if I am not). Let it be a merman – a man with a large fishy tail. I give a great swish with my tail – that is the night before – and then I find myself with a dazed mind and unfamiliar hands trying to get a firm grip of a slippery rock, fairly grounded in no-man's-land, where my tail doesn't work and my hands are a great deal less useful than a good earthy pair of hands would be – that is the morning after. A stranded merman! A most unconvincing beast!

Well, well, I say to myself: I *was* in the sea. Indubitable. And I *am* on the – no, that's just what I do not say. No, that I cannot really admit. I don't always go about challenging reality: when a motor-'bus makes for me, I get out of the way. When I want tobacco I put my money down and pick up my change; and I speak politely to policemen. I behave circumspectly, and try to dissemble my tail in a pair of trousers – even a pair of spats when I am feeling a peculiar need of protective colouring. But I do not really admit all these things. I feel that I have been pushed on to a stage, where I must behave like a little gentleman. But somewhere in my heart I cherish a secret conviction that the whole pasteboard contraption will vanish away.

In the meantime, with that grain of comfort, I wait for the tide to rise and cover me again. Next time, I say to myself, once I have the water fairly over me again, I will give such a flick with my tail as will carry me clean through the morning after, and the morning after that for ever and ever. And then, according to the theory of evolution, my useless hands will drop off, I shall grow scales to keep the water out, and I shall be no longer a hybrid merman, but a fish indeed, as Mr. Lawrence says I ought to be.

But I have not succeeded yet. I sometimes think that I am getting fishier and fishier, and that only my head remains unaffected. But it seems a very obstinate sort of head. The only thing that occurs to me to do with it is to bury it in the sand. I know that is what the ostrich does, and not the fish. But it's pleasant to welcome all these animals who come uninvited into the argument. Well, I put my head into the sand, in the hope that sooner or later it will come out something different. So far all that has happened is

that I have got a great deal of sand in my eyes. Yet
somehow it does not vastly matter, and I'm not sure
that it's not rather a good thing. When your eyes
are watering you don't see so very much; and it's very
good training for the moment, which will not fail to
come, when the tide is up and you are a fish again.
Your eyes are bound to smart in the one element or
the other; it is better that they should hurt you least
in the one you most delight in.

But it's all very well to try to laugh about these
things. One can't keep it up: at least, I can't. It is
not that this division into the night before and the
morning after is flippant but that it is too simple. It
suggests that there are, in fact, only two worlds to
deal with. I begin to suspect that there may be a
hundred or more. Or, if we go back to our merman
and fishes — for I am not enough of a realist to like
'the night before' or 'the morning after' — I have an
uncomfortable presentiment that there are not merely
the dry land and the ocean and the foreshore between
them on which I mostly live, but as many different
oceans as there are fishes to swim in them. For instance, when the waters seem to have covered me
indubitably and I begin to swim about with a sensation of speed and ease that is positively alarming, the
chances are that somebody else whom I have been
accustomed to regard as a perfect fish, instead of

admiring my beautiful evolutions as I expect him to or at least acquiescing in them, suddenly changes into an unmitigated land-animal, and begins to beat me about the head with his walking-stick. He is angry, and he shouts at me: 'Don't make such a damned fool of yourself! Can't you *see* what a spectacle you are? If you don't leave off this instant, I'll have done with you for ever.' And at the very moment when I think I am doing something superlative, some dolphin-roll that took an unusual amount of courage, he smites me with a quite special vehemence, and cries: 'Really, you make me sick!'

So I shake the sand out of my eyes and discover myself there in the old attitude, floundering on the beach, in the middle of an unpleasant sandy mess I have been churning up with my tail. Can that be all really? Am I nothing more than a monster in a circus? It is a very nasty moment. One goes all sick inside, but sick, sick, and death is near and desirable. Anything would be better; better than all else would be to close one's eyes and die, dreaming that one was a fish again.

Of course, I don't accept anybody's evidence as to what I am or the quality of my behaviour. Probably, all the inhabitants of the earthy world save one or two might beat me on the head for days together and roar at me through megaphones by the hour, and I should not turn a hair. I simply should not feel their blows or hear their voices. I at all events have got a tail, and I will not listen to those ordinary two-legged animals who would like to bully me. But, on the other hand, there are one or two people who, I believe, are fishier than I am; and, anyhow, what I believe or think in their regard is not of very much account beside the fact that when they speak to me it reverberates in my bowels. I cannot help it: the fact is elemental. I can only recognize it and obey.

So there I am: split clean in two, half of me still thinking I am a fish, half of me persuaded that I am only a circus-monster. It is indeed an unpleasant position, so very unpleasant that it is as well that this essay has been pitched in this minor key: otherwise I should be letting myself go and really making a spectacle of myself. The sense of nullity, of complete not-being that comes of such a split in the consciousness is purely nauseating. The ground gives way beneath you; you are falling, falling. Worse than that, for this ground on which you trod so securely was your own, painfully won. Your old brave words echo sickeningly in your ears. 'Obey no spiritual authority but your own.' Easy to say; hard to follow: for the voice from outside which you recognize as authoritative *is* your own. 'Be loyal to your own certainty.' But there are two certainties, in conflict, and they are both your own. 'When in doubt, do the hardest thing.' There is nothing to choose between them. It is just as hard to pretend you are a fish with that voice ringing — not in your soul, for that has slipped through the chasm — in your depths, as it is to admit that you are merely a circus-monster beside himself. Either way, something snaps.

And you, poor fool, had thought the time had come — had you not waited for it, had you not paid for it? — when you could trust yourself as a single thing. You had, by innumerable lonely pains, metamorphosed yourself into a fish. Now you realize that, although your outward shape has changed, you are still the hybrid that you were; your inside is a merman's still. You are — just what you were when you began, so many years ago. The mists of illusion begin to clear, and you see through them the old familiar situations with which you struggled when you first began to struggle at all. Nothing has changed but the suddenness and immensity of the shock. That, it seems, has increased a thousand times: but that also may be an illusion.

So, in the depths of your dismay, it will appear. And yet, perhaps, if you could be still and look more closely, you would find that something indeed had changed: that there was less of an old weak self-assertion about it all, that as your sacrifice was more of a sacrifice, your choice was more of a choice, and that, when it came to splitting yourself, you were more prepared to let the split go clean through.

Small comforts at the best; but small comforts are better than none.

At least, I suppose they ought to be. But when you have got into the position of not being able to make head or tail of yourself, grains of comfort are oddly intangible and unsustaining. You require something far more substantial, nothing less, indeed, than the assurance of a miracle: that next time your head will really come along with your tail, and be a proper fish's head, or that your tail will come along with your head and turn into a sensible pair of legs, fit for standing on. For the difficulty of standing on your head is nothing compared with the difficulty of standing on your tail. On the only occasion of which I know when that miracle was accomplished, the world was saved by it.

'Once upon a time all the water in the world was swallowed by a huge frog. It was most inconvenient, especially for the fishes, who flapped about and gasped on the dry land. The other animals also were troubled, because there was nothing to drink. So they laid their heads together and came to the conclusion that the only way to make the frog disgorge his waters was to make him laugh. Accordingly they gathered before him and cut capers and played pranks which would have caused any ordinary person to die of laughing. But the frog did not even smile.

He sat there in gloomy silence, with his great goggle eyes and his swollen cheeks, as grave as a judge. As a last resort the eel stood up on its tail and wriggled and danced about, twisting itself into most ridiculous contortions. This was more than even the frog could bear. His face relaxed, and he laughed till the tears ran down his cheeks and the water poured out of his mouth. However, the animals now got more than they bargained for, since the waters disgorged by the frog swelled into a great flood. Indeed, the whole of mankind would have been drowned, if the pelican had not gone about in a canoe picking up the survivors.'

That is the story as Sir James Frazer tells it. So you see, first, how hard it must be to stand on one's tail; and, secondly, that although in this great instance it brought salvation, the remedy was within an ace of being too heroic altogether. Therefore it is better not to try.

In short, at the present moment, I do not know what advice to give to those of the merman breed. Perhaps the farmer's wife — Magna Mater — could be found to cut off their tails with a carving-knife; if she were to cut off their heads by mistake, it would not greatly matter. But that is too drastic: I am gentle by nature, and particularly gentle to those of my kind. I would rather suggest a sun-cure. Let them bask on a warm rock, and go to sleep in the sunshine. It is a pity we can't all afford that: for sometimes I think that half our maladies are due to the fact that for most of the time the England we live in is like the bottom of a dingy aquarium. And we behave accordingly.

(*January*, 1924.)

The Two Worlds

IN 'HEADS OR TAILS?' I BEGAN TO DIS-
cuss, rather cavalierly perhaps, the problem of the
two worlds. It is, though it may not have appeared
so in my exposition, a fundamental and eternal
problem. Anyone who tries to live *his* life, who
struggles to possess a being of his own and to discover an allegiance which he cannot deny, is faced
with it over and over again. To-day it is probably
more insistent than ever. There are many reasons for
that. How you formulate them will depend upon the
degree to which, at the moment, you are accepting
the world without. If you are trying to take count
of it, you may be able to see the conjuncture of things
in which we are now involved as part of a secular and
recurrent historical process; and, by comparing kindred disquietudes in the past, you may even establish
it as a law of human action that at all times of profound social disturbance the emphasis shifts from the
world without to the world within. It is easy to see
why it must be so. In times of social upheaval mankind tends to act as a mass, and the individual who
because he is an individual must refuse to behave as
an atom in a mass, suddenly discovers that there is an
abyss between his realities and those of his fellow-
men. In the time before he had assumed that the
values of his world were the values of his fellows;

that honour and truth and justice meant the same things for all men. In a painful and blinding flash of illumination it is revealed to him that his faith was peculiar to himself: he had thought himself a member of a nation, in reality he is (at most) a member of a tiny sect. And still, in spite of all disillusion, this inward world of his remains real: he cannot deny it, for it is the only world in which he can live. So he is forced, for his own life's sake, to recoil into himself and to regard the world without as somehow not quite real, not really real.

This reaction has occurred again and again in human history; and there is good reason for supposing that it is more widespread and more violent now than ever before. Mankind had never been so much a herd as it was during the war, and so it has never behaved much as a herd as it has behaved after the war. Civilization has spent the best part of two hundred years in triumphantly binding the ends of the earth together. Two hundred years ago Carlisle was as far from London as San Francisco is to-day. During those two hundred years loosely united peoples have been imperceptibly welded into masses by the railway, the telegraph, and the penny post. And in the time of crisis they have behaved accordingly. The greater the action, the greater the reaction; the more threatening the mechanization and inertia of the world without, the more peremptory and exclusive, in those individuals who are sensitive to the menace, the insistence upon the superior reality of the world within.

I do not know whether this dispassionate historical view of the situation will bring so much comfort to my readers as it brings to me. I like to look before and after, though I pine for what is not. I see, as I look backward over the legible record of human destinies, the marks of the eternal discrepancy, now breaking into open and undisguised hostility in times of stress, now fading into the faint traces of individual suffering in times of social security. And I take comfort from the fact — or what appears to me to be a fact — that whenever the stress has become unbearable, and the disruption of an old order has begun, it has always been those who have insisted on the superior reality of the world within who have carried the living spark of a new order into the times after them. The spark has blazed and become the fiery heart of a new dispensation; then it has flickered, finally it has become a smouldering ash. And new rebels have arisen to fan it into flame once more.

But this long view, though it is comforting, does not practically settle the problem of the two worlds. That is, for any individual man, altogether more intimate and disquieting. He is, by force of circumstance and the necessity of the times, compelled to deny the claims of the world without to full reality.

He is driven more and more to build upon the reality of the world within, until one fine day he allows an act of his to be determined by it. That is to say, he attempts to manifest in the external world in obedience to an authority created by ignoring the external world. For he is not a Stoic, who saves himself a great deal of trouble by pretending that the world without is so unreal that we can have nothing to do with it: which is like shouting to an omnibus that it doesn't exist and then stepping out of its way. And he cannot by nature be an Epicurean. No, he tries to act. There comes a moment when he really does step in the way of the omnibus. If he escapes with his life he is lucky, and with his returning consciousness he realizes that he has been treating a solid reality as a dream.

So over he goes to the other side. He grits his teeth and determines to become one of 'those for whom the visible world exists.' It is more easily said than done. In a second he realizes, as of course he had realized before, but now more consciously and completely, that if he were to regard the world without as a real reality and to wear the fact of its objective existence as a frontlet between his eyes in all his feeling and thinking and scheming and doing, he would not feel or think or scheme or do anything at all. The inertia which confronts him would become an obsession. The conditions which he has to accept before he can begin to work upon it — and the chief of these conditions is to regard his fellow-men either as machines or part of the brute creation — fill him with horror. If he were to accept them, he would die; his springs of action would be paralyzed. So there is a solid brick wall in front of him. He may spend his time thumping his head against it if he likes. But the brick wall will last longer than his head.

So back he goes again. 'The visible world does not exist,' he whispers to himself once more. He keeps it up for a day or two. And once again he begins to acquire confidence and to behave as though the visible world really did not exist. He puts his head down and runs. Smack! It is the brick wall, once more, just as hard and apparently just as permanent as ever.

Now quite obviously he can't go on doing that. His head won't stand the strain. For the moment perhaps the best thing to do is to hoist himself on to the top of the wall, like Mr. Discobolus, and attend to his bumps and survey the scene. It is a vast one. All human life and all human history is contained between those brick walls he has encountered. It is only one brick wall, really, as he now sees, and it girds the human universe in a circle. There is a certain pleasure to be got out of a bird's-eye view. He sits, perched on top, quietly taking in the prospect, and thinking. What are his thoughts? Something like these.

The discrepancy, the downright opposition, between the world within and the world without must be accepted. He must also accept the fact that he belongs to both of them. There is really no point in going on banging away until his head splits into pieces, or swells so big that it can contain within itself the wall and the universe and every other mortal thing besides: he doesn't want to be discovered, as poor Nietzsche was discovered, signing letters: *Nietzsche Caesar*. That would be the end. On the other hand, he simply cannot accept the external world as it is. The terms are altogether too onerous — suffocating, unnatural, and poisonous. Just as surely, that is also an end. He was not made to regard his fellow-men as lumps of meat or movable dynamos; neither was he made to sit apart in cynical detachment. He was made otherwise, and his value, if he has any value, is that he *was* made otherwise.

What is to be done, then? He accepts the external world. What is he going to do with it? Run away from it? There is no objection provided he admits to himself what he is doing; and if he does admit it, he knows that it is only a temporary solution, a shelving of the importunate problem which will return again and again, until ultimately he acknowledges that his only way is to change, or try to change, the face of the external world. A tall order, that! Taller still because he knows that Beelzebub is the only name by which he can cast out Beelzebub. But conceive the miracle possible. By the time his impulse has filtered down in a universal and visible action, it is a monstrous caricature of what it was. 'Ah!' sighs the Quixote in him, 'one man's preaching sent the Kings of Christendom to win the Sepulchre of Christ from the infidel.' 'Oh!' cries the Sancho Panza, 'and what were the Crusades in fact but licensed looting? And modern French plutocratic Imperialism is all that remains of the Revolutionary idealism; and the mechanical Lenin was the omnipotent impresario of the dreams of generations of Russian political martyrs.' When it really comes to the casting out of Beelzebub, it is Beelzebub who does the work.

So he gives up the idea of changing the face of the world. If he could change a tiny corner of it – a single eyelash on that sphinx-like countenance – he would have some air to breathe, room to move, freedom to live his life, and he could believe that the little flame he kept alive would one day grow into a light to lighten the world. Perhaps not a very kindly light. One of the troubles of the world of late has been that the light has been much too kindly, nourished out of the purest wax and the most refined oil, so that none of the vast sensual realities of the world have attained their consummation in it. They have accumulated elsewhere until after years of smouldering they burst into a lurid glare that made the light apparent for what it was — an irrelevant and futile taper. No, the spark that must be lit and guarded in his changed corner of the world must have more flame than light about it. The eternal fire on the vestal hearth was a truer symbol than the undying candle of the Church. Fire consumes and transmutes; light throws a veil of appearance and leaves all things unchanged.

But a sense of proportion has descended upon him. He is not going to revolutionize the world. Is there then nothing he can do? What he can do is to try to create a nucleus, to gather together a sort of brotherhood, to build a milieu for himself, wherein his beliefs and aspirations shall find an echo and a response. And this time (such is his vow) the quality of the impulse must not be suffered to be degraded by the mechanism of its own expression. He dreams of a community whose force shall be measured not by the numbers of its professed adherents, but by the intensity and spontaneity of their devotion to the work before them: work on themselves, and work on the world without, shaping some small fragment of it into harmony with the world within. And it will be no sickly society of self-sacrifice; but a disciplined and aggressive body, a compact and agile fighting organization, which will do what it has to do resolutely, but with a sense of the fun of the thing. It will not go crawling around with its hat in its hand asking rich men to supply funds in the sacred name of art, or philanthropy, or the higher life, or any other sentimental bunkum; and it will not go hanging round politicians in the hope of sharing their kind patronage, or of making them see the light.

It is a fascinating dream. But being of a sceptical turn, he spends a day or two thinking it over. One of his great troubles is that he combines a good deal of personal experience of head-bumping with a good deal of accumulated knowledge of the arch-head-bumpers in the past. He knows the longing of the isolated individual to find others to share his faith – to be convinced by the fact of their belief of the reality of his own. Well, what of it? After all, and in spite of all, we do not, we cannot live alone. We do need a Church: but we have to insist on founding new ones. We want our Church, not *the* Church. And anyone who starts a magazine, if he does not aim at personal profit and is not indulging his personal vanity, is just as surely as the New Adventist preacher at the street-corner, trying to establish a new Church – a society of people who take seriously the things that he takes seriously and so far share his faith. And so is every writer who tries to put all he has and is into what he writes; he too is looking for disciples and fellow-members. This is what I believe; who will believe in what I believe? There is nothing to be alarmed at in this.

But then comes the further question: What *does* he believe in? Now, surely, it must be formulated. Now, surely, he is hoist with his own petard. He who inveighed against creeds and formulations, must produce a creed himself. But must he? Why should he produce clauses to which one must subscribe? Why not let it go at something less ambitious?

'I believe in — Religion, though I don't see very much of it — in Truth, which is even rarer — in Sincerity, which isn't achieved by everyone — in the value of certain individual persons who have had the courage of the truth that was in them which they gained by facing life for themselves — I believe in Heroes of humanity, and I think it would be a good thing if people could be made to understand them for what they were instead of paying lip-service to the mere phantasma of their names. But it doesn't seem to me to matter very much at this moment what I believe *in*. A few of the things that I believe would be more to the point. I believe that modern civilization is irremediably rotten: and that no political parties whether High Tory or Low Labour will produce any essential change; simply because the malady from which it suffers is too radical. It has no living heart; it is just a damnable, monstrous, stupid machine; and it turned into this while no one was looking and there is no turning it back again. And as for the wise men who want to hurry it forward, with their knowing air of omniscience, into a more perfect machine into which everything and everybody goes in equal and comes out the same only more so, I could wring their silly, crowing necks. They make me sick. And if you ask me what I offer in the place of this thing I despise and loathe — well, I don't know. I think the thing will slowly run down. All that seems to me to matter very much is that there should be a body of people who really don't care whether it does run down, who have attained, through a sufficiency of head-bumping, some sort of individual being and with it enough delight in the battle to be willing to take a few risks for the sake of creating something outside and apart from the machine. It is not, and it will not be, easy to get away from the machine. It has bitten pretty deep into most of us, and we are more than half-machines ourselves. Logically, we should deal with ourselves, each man with himself, first. But probably we shall have to let the logic go, and do what we can while we last.'

(February, 1924.)

Why Do I Write?

SOME ONE HAS WRITTEN TO ME TO effect. 'You talk of isolation, of living to one-self; you say: "Why should I waste my time any more, proclaiming that I am I?" Why then do you write? Isn't what you have found, or what you say you have found, sufficient?'

Why do I write? There are a good many answers to the question; and I feel it is one worth answering. But no more than feel it, for when I begin to write I never know what I am going to say. I am like a prospector who, when he sees a promising hole in the rock, strips and begins to dig furiously. He does not know what he is going to turn up. But for some reason or other this question seems to me a promising hole. One of the reasons is that it is so simple; another that it took me so much aback when I read it. Simple, disconcerting questions are good to answer: good, not in the sense of pleasant – they are mostly unpleasant – but in the sense of good for one's soul.

Why, then, do I write? And the answer must be 'dead honest,' as a friend of mine used to say – 'cross your heart straight dinkum.' Well, the first honest answer that comes to me is that I write because I *am* a journeyman. Writing is my trade, which I practise for a living. I try to write as well as I can, and as truly as I can, because I believe writing is an honourable and – yes, I will say it – a sacred craft. To be insincere as a writer is, in the long run, spiritual suicide. So that, although it is true that I write in the first instance because I was (by my own choice) brought up to the trade, it would be untrue to say (what the cheap cynic would suggest) that I write for money. I write for my living, simply, which is a different thing. That is to say, I would rather get three pounds for saying what I want to say than thirty for saying what I don't want to say.

So much for that. But, though it is a true answer, it is also a superficial one. I must get to something more essential. That is, as it were, the very outside skin of the onion. I am far from its centre of virtue and its source of tears. For what would I do if, being a journeyman, I suddenly found that I had nothing more to say: that the activity of writing had, in fact, become a mere automatism? I am afraid that would not deter me, because being what I am, and enjoying the freedom I enjoy in these pages, I should in all sincerity avoid the issue. I should immediately begin to inquire into the question why the source had failed – and if I could find no answer, inquire into the question why I could find no answer – and so *ad infinitum*.

That also gives no adequate reply to the question, Why do I write? Perhaps I have a better chance of pinning myself down if I turn the question inside out, and ask myself, Why do I not leave off writing? It is certainly not because I have to live, for though it is true that writing is the easiest and most natural means of making a living that I possess, I think I should have no difficulty in giving it up to-morrow if I began to feel that what I have to say is not worth saying. But perhaps in the very nature of things that moment can never come; perhaps I am really so much of an egotist that I cannot imagine a condition in which a truthful record of some thought or feeling of mine, even if it were no more than a feeling of utter weariness, would not be of some interest to somebody.

Indeed it seems to me, if I judge from my own experience, that there is always a certain interest and a certain value in a truthful record of a man's thoughts and feelings. How much good it has done me, in the past, to learn that some writer whom I admired had been at the end of *his* tether! To know that he, too, had days which were 'a weariness and a heaviness,' that he, too, behaved like a fool, that he, too, was childishly happy because his friend suddenly took him by the arm and said, 'I don't know what it is, old chap; I know you are a fool and all that — but I can't get over this absurd feeling of affection for you' — or something of that kind. To find that little preposterous things which have meant a great deal to us, have meant a great deal also to men far greater than we; to know that our heroes were troubled as we are troubled — this helps us towards that desired of all desirables: the courage of ourselves. How vividly I remember the moment when I first read in the Confessions how young Rousseau threw a stone at a tree, and felt that his future, his destiny, everything, depended upon his hitting it! How I loved him that day! Or when Tchehov in his letters tells of the pride with which he drove his cart from Melihovo to the station: how he drove furiously like Jehu, shouting all the way. When I was younger than I am now, such things as these had an immense importance for me. They lifted, each one a little, from me the nightmare horror of being abnormal and queer that used to brood over me. Not that one ever gets rid of the nightmare altogether, for there is a sense in which anyone who *is* anything at all is queer and alone for ever and ever. But the knowledge that there have been other queer and lonely ones is a very present help in trouble. I myself have got through some very nasty places by thinking of that queer fish Stendhal writing 'Yesterday I was fifty' on the *inside of his braces*!

And so it seems to me that it is possible, in one's turn, to make life a little easier for other people, simply by saying, 'This thing or this has been worrying me of late,' or 'This little thing has made me happy.' Not that I sit down with my pen with the idea of doing good. That only occurs to me when I think about what I am doing as I am thinking now. For the most part my only conscious motive is to satisfy this intermittent impulse which I have to write in a way that is compatible with my dignity as a human being: a dignity which demands that one should tell no lies either to oneself or to others. Because of that, and because of the act of writing seems to me the highest of human activities, I make it my business to express in the most intelligible language I can command the thoughts and feelings which are most real to me. That does not mean that I always want to be serious. Sometimes, I do not *feel* serious at all. And I can see no good reason for pretending to a seriousness which I do not feel.

But still I have not really faced the question, in the terms and in the intention of my questioner. For what he really means, I take it, is to ask — or to cause me to ask myself — whether the activity of writing is not somehow incompatible with my profession of faith in standing alone. Well, in the absolute sense, I think it is. Writing is essentially a sharing, *a communication*, of the writer's thoughts and feelings. If he stood alone absolutely, he would abstain from this communication. But he would also be a monster. To be anything absolutely is to be a monster, for it means that a human being is trying to disregard the conditions of his own humanity. Life is a compromise. It is based on the most astonishing compromise the human imagination has ever dreamed — one, indeed, that it never could have dreamed — the working arrangement between soul and body. They are perpetually at war, yet somehow they agree, somehow they know that each depends upon the other. And that fundamental conflict, occasionally resolved into harmony, prescribes the limits within which all human achievement must be bounded. This is, as it were, the rhythm which must govern all human activity. It emerges, in a thousand variations, in every corner of the great pattern of life. Thus, to stand alone absolutely is to be, or to try to be, all soul, for in this relation the rest of humankind are the body. If you sever your connection with the body, you die — you may explode in an imposing and incomprehensible blaze perhaps, but still you die. If you merge yourself in the body and sever your connection with the soul (which is your individual, indefeasible *self*), you also die. Standing alone, therefore, is relative. The most lonely man on earth sought disciples. And more, standing alone is only a means towards a communion that will not fail. It is a procedure, a technique, a way, by which the individual may fit himself for some new and richer and more stable relation with his fellows than the modern mechanism now permits.

With this final end writing is not incompatible. Far from it. The extremest individualist, by declaring his faith through the written word, declares something beyond his faith: he declares that he is, after all, a member of a society. Not of this one, perhaps, but of a society that may be.

(February 1924.)

I HAVE BEEN TO SEE MR. SHAW'S
Saint Joan three times within a week, and after the
third it seems to me that I know no more what to say
of it than I knew after the first. It is deeply moving
and it moves deep, very deep. Therefore one has
nothing to say about it, or everything. All that one
has thought or felt or dreamed or believed concerning the problem and the meaning of human life is
stirred into wakefulness by it. To criticize it a whole
creed, to expound it a whole philosophy is necessary.

Is that to say it is a great work of art? I do not
know, and do not greatly care. But it is to say that
it has the essential of a very great work of art, and
that it is, beyond all odds, the finest play that has
been produced upon the English stage within my
memory. I have two standards of reference in judg-
ing drama: one is a performance of *Othello*, the other
a performance of *The Cherry Orchard*. *Saint Joan*
moved me, differently indeed, but not less than they.
What can I do but declare my opinion that *Saint Joan*
in essence belongs to the same order as they? I could
concoct a niggling criticism of it, I could say that this
joke seemed to me rather cheap, and that embellish-
ment a little out of harmony: but how trivial and unprofitable! And how false to my immediate experience, which is that for three nights I have been held

spell-bound and on the brink of tears throughout three hours and more!

At first, thinking it over, I said to myself: Ah, but Mr. Shaw could not help it. He has triumphed in spite of himself. He had but to tell the story of Joan of Arc to rend our hearts with pity and terror. It is the eternal story of the Crucifixion: there is no difference. Christ's 'My God, my God, why hast thou forsaken me?' and Joan's 'My voices have deceived me,' were the cries of the same heart stricken by the same wound. 'Then all the disciples forsook him and fled': the very King of France whom she had crowned and the princes of the Church who had blessed her were silent during the six long months of her solitary trial. There is but one real difference: it is this. Christ had no one to call upon in the hour of his defeat: the Maid had Christ. More than six times at the stake she called upon his name, and the captain of the lonely ones received her into his bosom. The story had but to be told. Who could resist it?

Fool that I was! I should have asked rather: Who could tell it? As if I did not know that these miracles are not the work of every Tom, Dick, and Harry who supplies the ravenous machine of the London theatre with something to go on with. As if I were not old enough to have learned that the feeling: Ah, with such a story one could do anything, is the surest sign that the work which arouses it is a great one. As if I

234

did not know that the story of Joan of Arc had lain there ready for the handling this hundred years, that good men and true like Charles Péguy have tried their hands upon it and failed, and that even Anatole France's famous book is but a suave and careful repository of facts compared to Bernard Shaw's revivification of the thing that was. Let us be honest: the true relation between the *Vie de Jeanne d'Arc* and *Saint Joan* is much more like the relation between North's *Plutarch's Life of Antony* and Shakespeare's *Antony and Cleopatra* than it is to the relation between the work of a master and the work of a pupil, as our learned critics insinuate. The *Vie de Jeanne d'Arc* is a work of history: *Saint Joan* is a creation.

I am not criticizing Anatole France, and I know it is an exaggeration to compare North's *Plutarch* (which, for all its splendour of language is a childish thing) with the French master's subtle essay in historical criticism. Nevertheless, Shaw's work of re-creation, his re-shaping of the more complex and reluctant material of the life of Joan of Arc is, I believe, quite strictly comparable to Shakespeare's re-creation of Antony or Coriolanus. These things have a trick of looking simple – when they are done. But if the people who make these easy criticisms would spend a month or two in the vain effort to work the like miracle upon the like material – there are plenty of Plutarch's Lives left for our modern Shakespeares to transmute – they might be a little more forthcoming in their praise of those who accomplish it. There have not been many of them: so few indeed that we can be bold with safety and call the one play-wright we have who *can* work the miracle by his right name: a dramatic genius.

When we have something to praise, let us praise it. One would have thought from the criticisms of *Saint Joan* which came my way that Mr. Shaw had done quite well – unexpectedly well, in fact – in that he had followed in the footsteps of a master and not utterly misbehaved himself. That was the suggestion I drew from the dramatic critic of *The Times*: the others I read were less readable and rather more superior.[1] I saw the play, and began to wonder whether they had really read the *Vie de Jeanne d'Arc* of which they talked so much. After all, critics are hard-worked: they have to bluff occasionally. Ana-tole France makes a superior stick to beat Bernard Shaw with; and the superior public is just as gullible as any other – rather more so, in fact, for the inferior public generally does like what it says it likes, while the superior public spends half its time saying it likes what it doesn't like and hasn't read. 'Not so good as Anatole France.' 'Nothing like so subtle, *of course*.'

[1] I except absolutely from this condemnation Mr. Desmond McCarthy's article in *The New Statesman* of April 5.

I have heard it already, and I shall hear it many times again.

Bunkum! Shaw's *Saint Joan* is better than Anatole France's, and more subtle, and more true. Why, if Shakespeare had created a Master de Stogumber out of the bare word that the Earl of Warwick's chaplain abused the Bishop of Beauvais for accepting Joan's recantation – and it is the kind of thing Shakespeare used to do in his so different way – we should be breathless with admiration. So, for a change, let us be breathless here and now and not wait for our great-great-grandchildren to be breathless on our behalf. And as for subtlety, *Saint Joan* is triumphant. To have presented through a dozen different visions the fundamental truth of Joan's tragedy: to have shown how the principalities and powers of this world must inevitably be arrayed against one who makes the overwhelming claim that she made with the candour of utter simplicity and all the force of invincible faith – the claim to hear the voice of God: to have shown how the wise of this world must inevitably reject one whose wisdom is of another: to have shown how the Maid must be cast aside by the noble as a revolutionary, by the prelate as a heretic, by the English patriot as a witch, by the soldier as a charm whose potency is departed with her capture, by her own 'unpretending' king as an edged tool too dangerous for common use: to have shown that men, just because they are men, must forsake such a one, and that she can be truly followed only as followed her dear captain Christ, with the same faith to the same end: to have made this tragic truth so plain that he who runs may read, to drive it home into the hearts and minds of the hundreds who fill the New Theatre every night – needs more than extraordinary subtlety: it needs genius besides.

But more important still, I believe that *Saint Joan* is *truer* than the *Vie de Jeanne d'Arc*. Anatole France's creed is not adequate to his theme. He is a rationalist through and through. For him Joan is a charming, naïve, innocent peasant girl who dreams dreams, a pathetic and deluded visionary who distorts the secret promptings of her heart into the voices of God and his angels: in a word, she is mad. The attitude is a safe one; perhaps it is the only safe one. It is certainly the attitude the world has *acted* upon, and will act upon again, far less charitably than Anatole France. But it is not the attitude that men have lived by, and will continue to live by. The memory of Joan of Arc, and her greater Captain whom she followed, feeds an incessant hunger in the hearts of men: if they cannot act by such examples, neither can they live without them. What men cannot live without is as real as that by which they act. Life is not all action: if it were, the world would be the monkey-house it sometimes seems to be. We know better

238

than that: though what we know better and how we
know it would be hard to say. But dreams and desires and voices we cannot catch and Pisgah-sights
of lands we cannot enter are part of this knowledge
which lifts us out of the beasts that perish. And our
knowledge of Joan and her tragedy belongs to it also.
It is to us truly a tragedy, like the Crucifixion, like
Othello, like *The Cherry Orchard*; it is to us an evidence that life contains within it that which transcends
all mortal limitation – something beyond the knowing of our minds, but not beyond the reaches of our
soul. The story of Joan moves us to the depths, not
because it is patriotic, but because it is heroic, not
because she perished for a delusion, but because she
suffered for a truth. And a creed which has no place
for Joan's truth is inadequate to what she was; it
sinks beneath the level of her history.

Anatole France set out, urbane and humane, to
destroy the legend of Joan. There was plenty to
destroy in it: for she had been made the saint of a
church instead of a hero of humanity. There is no
private property in such a one as she. Her truth and
the meaning of her tragedy belongs to all the world.
The Church burned her, the Church has canonized
her, the Church has neither part nor lot in her save
in so far as it is an assemblage of men whose title to
her inspiration is simply that they are men. To
destroy the legend of the Church was one thing: to

destroy the legend of humanity another. Anatole
France did both. It was not his fault: those who
know his work know he is a Catholic at heart. He
cannot step out of the tradition into which he was
born, a tradition which says: There is an immutable
order of human things which man must know. In
that immutable order things are true or false: there
are no half-lights, there is no reality beyond the
knowable. For a mind of this tradition the issue is
simple, just as it was simple for Voltaire. The Church
is true or the Church is false: Joan is among the
saints, or Joan is among the mad. The Catholic tradition has no place for the isolated soul. That is why
it is a great tradition: it is based on the generality of
human experience, which is indeed that there is no
place for the isolated soul this side the grave.

But there is another tradition. It is that religion itself is an affair of the isolated soul, and that a man's
relation to God or to reality is the truer the less it is
mediated by institutions, or organized into creeds.
It is the Protestant tradition. In this tradition Joan
of Arc and the founder of her religion have their high
place; to this tradition Mr. Shaw himself belongs.
Therefore he understands the Maid as Anatole
France cannot understand her. For him she is not
mad: she is one of those who have had a glimpse of
what is beyond this mortal world. She is one of those
who move men's hearts not by exciting men's credu-

lity (as Anatole France would have it) but by kindling
the spark of the divine in them. 'When the spirit rises
up in her like that,' says Shaw's Captain La Hire
in Reims Cathedral, 'I could follow her to hell.'
Anatole France's La Hire would have had no such
moments of aberration – or inspiration. And here is
the real difference between the two Joans: Shaw's
Joan disturbs and inspires men by what she is, Anatole France's Joan moves them by what in their folly
they imagine her to be. In *Saint Joan* it is men's
secret wisdom that hearkens to her: in the *Vie de
Jeanne d'Arc* it is their invincible puerility that is
amazed.

Which is the truer? For me there is no doubt; 'j'ai
pris mon assiette.' When I read again Joan's verit-
able words in the narrative of Anatole France a
strange unease takes hold of me. In this setting they
are discordant: their strength and beauty, their swift
vitality is a deadly solvent of the framework in which
they are vainly held. The woman who spoke them
cannot be kept in the place assigned to her, for she is
manifestly a saint – but a saint not of a Church, but
of humanity. That there have been such I verily
believe, and that there will be again. The secret, the
spiritual flame which animates mankind is lit from
their achievements: the greatest poets, the greatest
painters, the greatest musicians belong to the same
succession, for they also, even though they are not

required to cast away their lives for them, have their voices which whisper an immortal truth to them and which they obey.

Bernard Shaw has risen to the height of his high argument. For my own part I could wish that the Epilogue were away. Here is his defence of it.

'The Epilogue' (he writes in the programme) 'is obviously not a representation of an actual scene, or even of a recorded dream: but it is none the less historical. Without it the play would be only a sensational tale of a girl who was burnt, leaving the spectators plunged in horror, despairing of humanity. The true tale of Saint Joan is a tale with a glorious ending; and any play that did not make this clear would be an insult to her memory.'

This is not true; and it is unjust to the play which he has written. *Saint Joan* is a tale with a glorious ending without the Epilogue, and it is Bernard Shaw's own art which has convinced us that it is so. To use the old, old phrase, we are purged by pity and terror – because we know the nature of the victim and that her death is inevitable. And it is the playwright who has made us aware of what she is and why her martyrdom must be. The glorious ending is there, as it is in all true tragedy. But tragedy is tragedy. To soften the impact of it is a mistake. The

Epilogue does not give the drama a glorious ending: it takes away from the glory of the ending which it has.

(*April*, 1924).

Postscript. In the preface to the printed edition of *Saint Joan*, Mr. Shaw once more defends the Epilogue, in these words:

' As to the epilogue, I could hardly be expected to stultify myself by implying that Joan's history in the world ended unhappily with her execution, instead of beginning there. It was necessary by hook or crook to show the canonized Joan as well as the inciner-ated one; for many a woman has got herself burnt by carelessly whisking a muslin skirt into the drawing-room fireplace, but getting canonized is a different matter, and a more important one. So I am afraid the epilogue must stand.'

The answer to this, it seems to me, is that the in-cinerated Joan *was* the canonized one. There is no point in the reference to the many women who have got themselves burnt 'by carelessly whisking a muslin skirt into the drawing-room fireplace': it is irrelevant, because Mr. Shaw has shown why and how inevitably Joan was burnt not by accident, but because she was what she was. *Saint Joan* is a great play precisely because it does show us this.

That she has been canonized may be important, but it is important as a matter of sociology. It adds nothing to her own import or to that of the play. The fact that in the year 1924 Mr. Shaw could take Joan of Arc for his heroine with the assurance that his audience would know roughly who and what she was, that he could go for his material to modern books in which every recoverable detail of her life and trial has been diligently examined and recorded – the fact in short that humanity has insisted on making her its heroine and keeping her memory alive – this is the fact on which the play is built. Her membership of the Catholic church and her ultimate canonization by it, are no more than accidental manifestations of a fact far bigger than they. All the implications of her canonization which are really essential to Joan's history are presupposed by the very conception of the play. Those implications of her canonization which are not presupposed by it are irrelevant, and somehow trivial.

And, I confess, this is the impression that the epilogue as a whole makes upon me. What is relevant in it, I have learned (and by the author's skill learned only too well) before: what is irrelevant in it is parochial and beneath the level of the universal tragedy I have been witnessing. I am suddenly made conscious of the presence of Mr. Shaw, and I am suddenly oblivious of the presence of Joan, although she

is in the centre of the stage and although the curtain
falls with the limelight full upon her. And I conclude,
not merely that with Joan's burning her story reached
its consummation, but that whereas Mr. Shaw, while
he had the actual facts of the history of the Maid
before him, submitted himself reverently to the spirit
he discerned in them, when the facts of the history
ceased, he became himself again. Mr. Shaw himself
is brilliant, but Mr. Shaw deliberately making himself the vehicle of a spirit greater than his own is more
than brilliant, he is impressive. *Saint Joan* is an impressive play, because through Mr. Shaw's instru-
mentality it is hers. Mr. Shaw's own part in the epilogue is brilliant, but it does not belong.

So that, when Mr. Shaw says 'I could hardly be
expected to stultify myself by implying that Joan's
history in the world ended unhappily with her execution instead of beginning there' I should reply that
it was precisely because that very personal thought
of whether he would or would not stultify himself
began to enter in, that the epilogue began to have a
tinge of unworthiness. There are certain things that
have to be left to make their own impression. True
tragedy is one of them. Those who do not understand it cannot be made to understand it. It needs
no underlining, and what is more, and more to the
point, it is incapable of being underlined, for no
human being is worthy to do it. And that is why, in

my opinion, Mr. Shaw has partly failed as an artist in the epilogue to *Saint Joan*. In those terms, he would no doubt laugh at the criticism. Art, he would say, does not bother him in the least. Neither does it bother me, but that is because I am persuaded that in the only sense of the word art that really matters to succeed as an artist is a moral triumph, and to fail as an artist is a moral failure. In *Saint Joan* there is much more triumph than failure. Were it not so, I should hesitate before declaring my opinion about the epilogue and Mr. Shaw's defence of it.

(*July*, 1924.)

The Well at Cerne

I HAD GOT OUT OF THE HABIT OF English winters. Suddenly, after avoiding them for three or four years, I was plunged into the longest that I can remember. It was like a long dark tunnel with a pin-point of light unimaginable miles away towards which the mere attempt to struggle was derisory. Fantastic thoughts came into one's head: plans of miraculous escape not merely into the sun, but into a region where sun and moon and stars have ceased to be. Anything seemed possible because anything seemed desirable; and rather than wake up again to that grudged and leaden dawn, it seemed better not to wake at all.

Work was the only remedy, I said to myself, a wall of preoccupation to shut out the menace of those coldly hostile skies. Within a week or two I found that there is no perennial source of energy within ourselves: whatever small fire we may possess is fed from without: the flame may be our own, but the fuel is not. And my flame much more nearly resembled a candle-light than it did the titanic blast-furnace which could have burned bright metal out of the grey rock of those days, or tempered that implacable north-easter in its crucible to a semblance of the warm vaunt-courier of the spring. How could one give out when there was nothing to take in? It was impossible; and the only perceptible result of self-seclusion in the tower of ivory — ivory in bulk is not a sympathetic or stimulating building-material — during weather in which to look out of the window was a weariness, was that one woke up in the morning far more tired than one had gone to sleep at night.

At such a moment, even one who is constitutionally averse to precautions begins to sit up and take notice. It is the signal for something sudden and drastic to be done. These things, if you are rich, are spectacular and expensive. My problem was to achieve the effect and spend no more than I should by staying at home. There were two of us: we would explore a county unknown to us: we would wander the length and breadth of Dorsetshire: we would camp out on the way. It was not spectacular, but it was both sudden and drastic, for the north-easter did not abate; it had even discovered an ally in a hideous mixture of snow and icy rain. 'You have to be hardened to these things,' said my companion moodily, 'or it's no good.' Neither of us had the inward conviction of being hardened to these things, so we waited till five days of our possible twenty had gone. Then, with the rain of the sixth morning, we lost patience. 'We'll risk it,' we said, and puffed out of London on a small traction-engine into the sardonic rain.

That evening the white south wind blew and cleared the sky: by the day after the sun had warmed the air,

and the next drop of rain that fell was on our home-
ward journey, when we welcomed it like an old friend
whom we had not seen for long. There is no need to
tell of our adventures: we had them, but the greatest
adventure of all was this: that we went out on the first
fine day and came home with the last of a brief inter-
lude of divine English weather that played to a climax
at Easter. Every night when we slept — or tried to —
and every morning when we woke, we murmured to
ourselves that God is good. Within a dozen hours
of our departure we had forgotten that London ever
existed, and we scarcely remembered it when we
returned. A hundred times we agreed in a kind of
maudlin ecstasy that it was worth having lived
through that winter to have had this unbroken plunge
into the dayspring of the year.

To have sat on a barren upland by the embers of
a woodfire with our foreheads touching the stars,
musing on nothing to the cry of the sad and restless
peewit and the droning of a ghostly snipe; to have
listened with fitful interludes of sleep all through one
night in the woodland to a nightingale trying her
reluctant song in vain —

'Whenas the new-abasshéd nightingale,
Stinteth at first ere she beginneth sing —';

to have stared from the heath above throughout
a cloudless day at the golden bow of Chesil Beach

249

swinging into nothingness at Portland's invisible Bill, while the sea beyond murmured a gentle, sleepy, caressing *A-a-a-ah*, then dully thundered a heavy menacing *A-a-a-ah*, then whispered a small faint and far away *A-a-a-ah*, very sinister, the manifest last word, and to have watched and listened till the end — a sombre but peaceful sunset, through bars of slaty cloud; to have lain through a grey afternoon on the turf bank of the innermost ring of Maiden Castle, looking lazily beyond the sheep to where the Roman Road flies 'like an arwè clere' westward out of Dorchester and wondering what manner of men they were who laboured that amazing rampart on the hill, and had no dream of the net of horrors their far posterity would weave about themselves — these things were good.

Dorset is old, but its age is friendly to man. On those hill-tops one is vexed by no vague memory of foul and forgotten doings, or of a knowledge which man has buried in his heart because it was better so, but which might awake to life again. Religion is there and the awe of religion: valleys and hills are steeped in sanctity: the presences — the *numina* — are powerful still, but they are kindly and not hostile. One sinks into them as Lazarus into the bosom of Abraham. When the monks came to the lovely valley of Cerne Abbas they did not come as outposts of light in a land of darkness: there was nothing to

250

exorcise, and even if they made a slow procession up the hill-side to sprinkle holy-water on the Cerne Giant, with his portentous emblem of an older faith than theirs, they let him bide. He was not really an enemy: they could accommodate him within their generous creed. They did not come to deny life, but to make what was crude in it more comely, to distil a peace and a wisdom out of a nature whose quiet indifference did not refuse them; they came to build a vessel to be brimmed for ever with the peace and wisdom they had distilled, as the spring they set about with lovely stones and deep-red bricks and the quiet of mighty trees flows for ever with water whose movement is music and its pureness a mystery.

To hold Dorset in a timeless moment, to be rapt into its immemorial spirit which abides, you have only to stand by the well at Cerne, and look and listen and be still. It is not hard to be still there. You pass through a quiet street, and into one still quieter where cobbles gently lose themselves in a pool of grass at the very door of the Abbey Farm: then through a gate into the churchyard with straight paths and cypresses to a little avenue of great soaring trees. A paved and grass-grown way slopes between them to the well. You hear nothing but your footsteps, and they are light, for the same spell which has fallen on your tongue has stilled your feet also. You cannot resist: the silence pours softly into your heart: in a moment, did you linger, you would hear the voice of command, but gentle and not fearful, from within and not from without: 'Put off thy shoes from off thy feet, for the place whereon thou standest is holy ground.'

And it is a holy place: as you walk down the slope, your head is bowed and your steps are slow as in procession. You are a small, not wholly worthy but wholly worshipping thing in the presence of this peace. The hands that made the basin for this perennial spring wrought in purity of heart and in patience: they were the hands of men whose souls were not disquieted within them, neither distraught by feverish and aimless doing, nor restless and tormented with the desire to burst through the limitations of humanity. The peace which is borne from them to you through the dissolving centuries, they possessed: and while you stand still by the well to partake of it more completely, while you make a peace in your body and soul in order that this greater peace may enter in and find a fit habitation, you listen to the running of the crystal water over the channelled stone. It is saying something – something which at this moment you understand, but will forget, which you have always known and never been able to utter – a melody by which if men could live only for a day the face of the world would be changed.

It is not for me to attempt to find words of my own

for that melody: it is enough that one can sometimes be still and hear it. To utter it in words is the privilege of the heroes of humanity: the great poets, the great painters, the great musicians catch an echo of it. It is most magically and most simply spoken, so that the child may understand, in the words of Jesus: it is what Walter Pater heard, what simpler men than he have heard, in the words: 'Come unto me, all ye that labour and are heavy-laden, and I will give you rest: for my yoke is easy and my burden is light.' It was all very well for the cultivated Victorian lady to urge the necessity of a complete agnosticism upon him. 'It's all very well,' said Walter Pater, as he repeated the words and nodded his head, 'but you can't explain that: there's a mystery.' And there *is* a mystery. And it's all very well for people who cannot hear this melody to say that the mystery is not there; and it's all very well for the wise of this world to assure us that works of art are all the same kind of thing: but quite simple people know that there are the poems and the music and the pictures which are touched with this mystery, and there are the poems and the music and the pictures which are not, and these latter can never haunt us as the former do.

This melody is sad and still and piercingly sweet. It touches with a sudden peace hearts which know, by that very touch, that they can never make it wholly theirs. We do not know from what it comes, but we say to ourselves that it is the sign of a great understanding in him who utters it, because it seems to hold the key to all perplexities. He must have suffered greatly, we feel, 'a man of sorrows and acquainted with grief,' and have come to understand that his sufferings and his sorrows were his privilege. For this melody, we know not how, sounds to us as the voice of acceptance: it is the sign that he who utters it has found the courage to look steadily at this strange and painful and lovely world and comprehend. Nor is this comprehension the privilege of the old; it is not the gift of years. Keats, who died at twenty-five, had found it, and he put perhaps as much of the mystery as any man has put in words in his vision of Moneta:

'Then saw I a wan face
Not pined by human sorrows, but bright-blanch'd
By an immortal sickness which kills not;
It works a constant change, which happy death
Can put no end to: deathwards progressing
To no death was that visage: it had past
The lily and the snow; and beyond these
I must not think now, though I saw that face.
But for her eyes I should have fled away;
They held me back with a benignant light,
Soft, mitigated by divinest lids
Half-closed, and visionless entire they seemed

Of all external things; they saw me not
But in blank splendour beamed, like the mild moon,
Who comforts those she sees not, who knows not
What eyes are upward cast.'

There, in those astonishing lines, is the symbol of the
poet's comprehension and acceptance.

Still closer to us, this acceptance is in those haunt-
ing late poems of Thomas Hardy called 'Veteris
Vestigia Flammæ,' and it is in the content and very
cadence of this entry in Anton Tchehov's note-book,
which no one who has ever read can forget:

'Essentially all this is crude and meaningless, and
romantic love appears as meaningless as an avalanche
which involuntarily rolls down a mountain and over-
whelms people. But when one listens to music, all
this is – that some people lie in their graves and sleep,
and that one woman is alive and, grey headed, is now
sitting in a box in the theatre, and seems quiet and
majestic; and the avalanche is no longer meaningless since in nature everything has a meaning. And
every thing is forgiven, and it would be strange not
to forgive.'

Of all the late-time utterers of this secret melody
Anton Tchehov is to me the most miraculous. Again
and again when I read him my throat aches with
tears, not of sadness or pity but of wonder at his

understanding, which takes the breath with beauty. And always, if I am required to explain to another wherein this beauty consists, I try to repeat that passage from the note-book; for the mystery of Tchehov is there.

And every now and then when I am off my guard, when some note is sounded in a conversation which breaks down my defences or some 'special instant is special blest' by a glimpse of the eternal newness of the visible world, that sentence of Tchehov's comes to take me unawares. 'And everything is forgiven, and it would be strange not to forgive.' It is like a strange jewel dropped from another world, and I find myself staring at it and trying to fathom the mystery of its enchantment. And sometimes it seems that I am near the secret, and sometimes far away: most near, perhaps, when I feel (as I feel now) that the secret is in the word 'strange.' Then my thoughts run somehow thus.

It would be strange not to forgive. Not: you *must* forgive. Simply, it would be strange not to forgive. If you did not forgive someone's eyes would glance at you with wonder, thinking you strange.

The glance of wonder! It is that, and that alone which will fly to the chinks of our armour. If it touches us, then we also in our turn begin to wonder, and it becomes an instinct that we should wonder when all is not forgiven.

What is to be forgiven? First, the evil that life has done us, our own suffering. That is hardest to forgive. Resentment has eaten so deep into us that it is part of ourselves; it is a wound in our back that we cannot reach to heal, a thing we cannot see to smile upon it. And we have to smile, because we have to forgive. Forgiveness is the smile of understanding: not resignation, not indifference: more even than acceptance – a simple and natural yea-saying. To do this we have to feel in ourselves that it would be strange not to forgive; we have to wonder at ourselves for not forgiving. If we could but wonder at ourselves for not forgiving, the miracle is accomplished: our hearts are turned.

Once there was a man who spent his life doing this miracle. He glanced with wonder at men and women who did not forgive other men and women, and above all, life; and when they caught his curious glance of wonder, they began to wonder at themselves for not forgiving. It is so extraordinarily simple; like all truly mysterious things, perfectly simple. Before they met him, people had thought it natural not to forgive, foolish perhaps to brood over injuries, but if you were made that way, why, the most natural thing in the world. The best thing (the wise among them thought) was to be resigned and indifferent. But to forgive, that was silly. To accept necessity, to bow the head and clench the teeth, that was wise, though it was not given to all men to attain wisdom. But to forgive! Nobody had thought of that. Or if they had thought of it, it must have seemed unnatural and inhuman.

Then came this man who found in himself that it was strange not to forgive; who, having wondered at himself for not forgiving and so found it simple to forgive, began to look with wonder at others. It's a very queer feeling when somebody simply wonders at you, not abuses you, or commands you, or even laughs at you. The power of laughter is great, but it touches only the social man; the power of wonder is tremendous, for it touches the spiritual man. . . .

I did not think all these thoughts (if thoughts they are) while I stood by the well at Cerne. I scarcely thought at all, for while you listen to the running of the water, you are at peace and reconciled: and in peace and reconciliation there is no room for thought. Only a dim yet potent memory of the souls who had wrought this peace which I had inherited, and made the hills and the trees and the sky enter into a league with their intention, so that when they were dust and their bells silent and their buildings waste, nature itself should whisper to anyone who paused to hear the words and the message of him whose faithful labourers they were. For while I stood and listened I was conscious of the power that had inspired them; I knew by what guidance they had chosen this lovely place which they made more lovely. The voice they heard was true: it has endured, and it will endure for ever — for surely the time will never be when there are no longer men who can wait, if not by the well at Cerne, by the pool of silence in their own hearts and declare to the world the music they have heard.

(May, 1924).

The Religion of Mark Rutherford

I HAVE BEEN READING THE NEWLY published volumes of Mark Rutherford's letters,[1] and I have been struck once more (for it is now a dozen years since 'Pages from a Journal' first wove their quiet spell about me) by the extraordinary 'quality' of the man – of the man rather than the mind or the work; for the first element to be insisted on, were one to attempt the almost impossible task of defining this 'quality,' would be the manifest oneness of Mark Rutherford. His letters, his novels, his journals, are radiations from a single living centre, functions – to use a mathematical term – of one unchanging soul. Unchanging, do I say? Unchanging, in the sense that all true organic growth is essentially contained in the seed from which it springs, or as the compass-needle through shocks and storms quivers always towards the pole. Unchanging, yet ever flexible, as must be the soul of a man who is wholly turned towards the discovery and the service of a living truth, and is sufficiently attuned to it to know that it will not be found in definitions, but rather in the note of a strange, still voice, which needs to be listened for, in men and works and the world.

Mark Rutherford, who could listen for the voice,

[1] *Letters to Three Friends.* By William Hale White. *The Groombridge Diary.* By Dorothy V. White. (Milford.)

could also use it. By the patience of his quest for truth, he became true. And we, in reading him, are made continually aware of this beautiful veracity: with what is true in ourselves we respond to it, and if that is our business, we try (as I am trying now) to communicate some sense of it to others. It is not easy: I grope for a word, and as sometimes happens, one recurs again and again to my mind. Mark Rutherford's writing is *suffused* with the beauty of truth. There is in him no brilliant, blinding flame; no flash of lightning; but a gentle and steady glow. And again this suffused light of his is somehow cool: though he struggled with questions which have fevered men, no trace of feverishness remains. Assuredly he had felt the fevers — for they are impossible to escape — but he waited for utterance till they were past. It was necessary to him that what he said should have the endorsement of his whole being, the imprimatur of his enduring self. Until that was given, his lips were locked.

To-day we begin to feel what is the reward of his impassioned integrity. (Impassioned may appear to some eyes a strange epithet for Mark Rutherford: but that will be because they do not see below the surface. Reticence like his is bought at a price: it is not, it is utterly different from, the conventional device of under-statement, with which amusing tricks can be played, but nothing more: this reticence is achieved only by a passion for true statement, by an unflinching suppression of the momentary ego in favour of the enduring self.) As he was single, his work also is single; the various parts cohere into one whole: and now that the turbid tides of popular applause and popular reaction which surged about the great figures of the nineteenth century have begun to ebb, Mark Rutherford's work remains, not gigantic, perhaps not even great, but secure against decay, because it was moulded by a true man after his own image. In his work, Mark Rutherford was himself, the more surely because he knew how hard a thing that is to be. He digged down to the bedrock in his soul, and his works rest unshakable upon that firm foundation.

He had many questions and no answers. Or rather he had one single and all-comprehending answer for which he could find no words; it lay so deep within him that he could not bring it to the surface, and because he knew how deep it lay he turned aside from the more facile surface-statements of conventional religion. 'Do I believe in God?' he said one day. ' There is nothing else in which I *do* believe.' And precisely because this belief of his was so profound and comprehensive, his God was truly ineffable; not to be uttered or defined, but to be felt and worshipped both in the world without and the world within. Such a God is not an answer to problems: were he to be an answer to them, he would become other than he is, for problems are the formulation by the partial human mind of the mysterious and simple reality of life with which the whole being alone can make contact. Mark Rutherford's belief in God did not help him to any philosophic reconciliation.

'There is so much unaccountable, undeserved misery in the world (he wrote in a letter of 1897), that I find the only thing to be done is not to think about it. I do not mean that we ought to refrain from thinking about the sufferer, but that philosophizing and attempts at reconciliation are useless. We must simply be silent, and not only be silent, but refuse to reflect upon the subject, and we must busy ourselves rather with what is productive of quiet content and joy. Every moment wasted on insoluble problems is so much taken from time which might be spent in the absorption of sunlight.'

Our first impulse is to contrast this declaration with the words which Keats put into the mouth of the goddess who guarded the shrine of the ultimate Truth:

'None can usurp this height (return'd that Shade)
  But those to whom the miseries of the world
  Are misery, and will not let them rest.'

But in reality there is no contrast. It is only the man 'to whom the miseries of the world *are* misery' who

263

can write as Mark Rutherford does. He is preaching to himself a counsel of perfection which he cannot obey: the miseries 'will not let him rest,' though he longs to rest. The man who has truly felt their torment, not as a mere dilemma of the intellect upon which he can indulge himself in speculation, but as a hidden throbbing wound in his soul, cannot turn aside to busy himself 'with what is productive of quiet content and joy.' This is what he longs to do, but cannot do: instead, he is driven onwards to discover the meaning of it all. And men like Mark Rutherford, and like Keats, do discover the meaning; only it is impossible for them to say wherein the meaning consists. For the reconciliation they achieve is not an intellectual reconciliation: if it were so, it would be easy for them to say wherein it consisted, and easier still for the next-comer with a pennyworth of dialectic from the schools to prove that their reconciliation was nothing of the kind. But the meaning which these chosen spirits seek and find evades their conscious utterance; it cannot be spoken. But it can be shown, it can be communicated. It is to be found in the very texture of Mark Rutherford's work: we make contact with it through his 'quality.'

When I think about him, and the men like him — and the greatest are like him in this — I wonder why it is so hard for some people to accept, or even to understand, the vital distinction: that the deepest things may be revealed, but may not be uttered. To have accepted that seems to me the beginning of wisdom, and the harbinger of peace. And yet, when I look about me, I see that those who are most vociferously adamant against this suggestion are often those who talk most loudly about Art, about the meaning and value and sacrosanctity of Art. I find it hard to understand how, if Art does indeed mean so much to them, they can be blind to the fundamental truth by virtue of which alone Art can be a mystery to be revered. Art holds the place it does in our secret loyalties — so it seems to me — because it does reveal what cannot be uttered. That, and no other, is the test of its authenticity. Does this poem, this picture, this piece of music convey to us some meaning which, we realize as we sense it, could be conveyed to us by no other means? If we can truly answer 'Yes,' then we are in the presence of the mystery of Art. I know of no other sign.

Certainly there are little mysteries and big ones, mysteries of Shakespeare and mysteries of Herrick, but all alike are members of the same mystery. And this hierarchy of mysteries must culminate in the mystery of God. I do not want to talk about God any more: I would be glad if I could, once and for all, banish the name from these pages. We do no good by talking about him, for though God, which is the name we give to the mystery and meaning of human life, may be revealed, he cannot be uttered. We do harm, we mislead, when we talk about him. He becomes an uttered God, who is either assimilated to other uttered Gods, or denied in the name of them. And in the clamour of the conflict between uttered Gods, the sense of the unutterable God, the maker of Heaven and earth and all that is therein, is frittered away and lost. But if, as I hope, the name of God will henceforward be banished from these pages of mine, let it be understood why he disappears: it is because when we utter him, we falsify him. The God we speak is not the God in whom we believe.

And sometimes lately I have thought (though it may be an impossible dream) that what the world is waiting for is union in the awareness and worship of the God who is ineffable. If men could only be content to allow what their liturgies describe as ineffable, to remain ineffable, – unspeakable and therefore unspoken, something would have happened to the mind and soul of man: they would be changed, and that change would mark a new epoch in the history of the spirit of man. It is because we insist on speaking the ineffable divine, on holding it in the grasp of the intellectual mind, on organizing it into systems and institutions, that troubles and disquiet begin. Against every formulation of the divine a counter-formulation is pitted: against a God of Love, a God of Cruelty is arrayed, and the opposing armies hurl against each other the charge of blasphemy. The opposition, and the waste of opposition, will go on and on; for opposition is inevitable, because these partial formulations are untrue. Against a God of Love a God of Cruelty *must* be pitted: against a God of Life a God of Death: for every utterance of the nature of the divine demands its opposite, lest the majesty and truth of the meaning be weakened.

It is not easy to forgo utterances and systems, into which, when we have our own certainty, we can pour our own meaning, and to which in the moments when certainty leaves us we can in some way cling. But surely it is far better, far more truly consonant with our human dignity, if certainty leaves us, to face the fact and admit to ourselves that we no longer know. After all, it is unlikely that having known the divine, we should be wholly deserted by our knowledge. What is far more likely is that if we have had the temerity to utter the ineffable, our utterance will be discomfited and brought to nought. In that case the truth of the matter will be not that the divine has deserted us, but we have deserted the divine: the meaning has not betrayed us, we have betrayed the meaning. We pay for our treachery by a sense of desolation and abandonment. It is far better to acknowledge the offence and understand the penalty than to turn for support and comfort where no enduring support or comfort may be found. This is not to propound a general rule. Probably there are those who cannot stand alone; but it seems to me that the spiritual hope of humanity rests chiefly on those who can. Of these Mark Rutherford was eminently one. Never was a man more profoundly religious than he; never was one more resolute in refusing to accept consolations which he did not feel to be true.

'I have been thinking much (he wrote to an old and dear woman friend of his in 1905) on one point of resemblance between my sister Henrietta and yourself. She never fell away into any artificial religion. She never believed that a supernatural creed was necessary for the training of children. The example of father and mother was, she knew, the only effectual religion for a child. I wish I could discover one or two more people of her temper. How you find it, I cannot say, but I see so many examples, especially amongst young women, of weak clutching at ceremonies and creeds and occasionally of perversion to extreme forms of Anglicanism. They have no strength of their own to stand without this poor and hollow support. It used to vex me and provoke opposition. It now merely saddens me and I hold my tongue, reflecting that it is an indication of what no argument can cure. If they are relieved by genuflexions and incense and candles, and if life becomes any simpler to them through doctrines of which they can give no intelligible account, I must not quarrel with them. So they are made.'

In that letter is revealed one aspect of Mark Rutherford's attitude: in order that hasty conclusions should not be drawn from it, here is another: —

'I think you would admit (I am sure I do) that at any rate the symbolism of Catholicism, as, for example, at Candlemas, is sometimes expressive of deeper truth than anything that can be put into words. Catholicism herein shows profounder insight than Protestantism into the nature of truth and of man. Catholicism knows what words cannot do. Protestantism struggles to put everything into words. The vital part of religion is wordless and purely symbolic.' (February, 1911.)

Contradictory? Inconsistent? I do not find them so: to me the underlying substance of both letters is the same instinctive aversion from the *utterance* of the divine. It is to be apprehended, experienced, lived, but not spoken.

Believing this, Mark Rutherford necessarily stood apart and alone. He could not do otherwise if he was to be loyal to his own sincere and characteristic profession: 'No religion is possible unless veracity lies at its base.' But the essential barrier between himself and the Churches may be seen from another angle and described in other terms. For although Mark Rutherford is rightly assimilated to those writers

269

who, like Keats, were made religious seekers by the imperious nature of their art, he differs from them in that he was saturated through and through in the tradition of Christianity. As readers of *The Autobiography* know, he was trained to the ministry of the Countess of Huntingdon's Connexion, and expelled from the training college for his refusal 'to slur over a difference between himself and his teacher on the subject of the inspiration of the Bible,' that is to say, for being more scrupulously Christian than his masters. To understand the exact quality of his religious belief it is therefore necessary to approach it in terms of his relation to Christianity. Mark Rutherford was primarily a follower of Christ, and like other followers of Christ who have the sympathetic imagination to understand their leader, he found an irreconcilable conflict between Christ and Christianity.

'I don't want to be egotistical (he wrote in December, 1901), but I will boldly affirm that even the parsons do not and cannot believe that there was as much God in Jesus Christ as I believe there was. Please observe the "cannot." The official theory absolutely prevents a true appreciation of the Divine in Christ.'

It would take too long to explain this last sentence to those who have no immediate sense of its meaning: one can only say that to Mark Rutherford it was necessary that Christ should be wholly and entirely human in order that the true splendour of his sacrifice and the full triumph of his tragedy should be manifest. Whether Mark Rutherford's judgment was at fault in imputing to all parsons an implicit belief in 'the official theory' is another matter: but a man who has abandoned the ministry because he refused 'to slur over a difference,' has the right to exact a like integrity from others. For Mark Rutherford the parson who did not accept the Church's theory had no place in the Church: by remaining in it he came under the ban of the first article of Rutherford's creed: 'No religion is possible unless veracity lies at its base.'

Christ on the one hand, then, and professed Christianity on the other. These were to Mark Rutherford distinct and opposite, as they were to Dostoevsky. The outbreak of the Boer War, the staring evidence of the utter lack of any true influence of Christ in the ordering of the nation's affairs, stirred him to this outburst of irony and despair.

'If you have the opportunity I wish you would ask the first clerical person you meet of what use Christianity is. I really begin to believe that it is not only of no use, but that if it could be swept out of existence we should morally gain by the disappearance with it of whole continents of cant. The great majority of the English people, excepting a few like the Quakers, the Bishop of Hereford, and the Dean of Durham, read and approve the *Daily Mail*, or the *Telegraph*, or the *Times*, and in so doing must put Christ in a cupboard and turn the key. They dare not look at Him and ask whether He would have approved this war. "Oh," but they will perhaps say, " what has Christianity to do with politics?" If it has nothing to do with politics or daily life it is not a religion. A religion is not a tangle of metaphysical subtleties nor a nostrum for preserving eternally the salt that keeps our carcases from putrefaction. Another possible excuse may be disagreement as to facts, but upon all that are important there is none. The real truth is that our so-called Christianity is the merest external film which the slightest bubble of passion or interest can wreck in an instant. Some good creatures, knowing in their hearts all that I have said to be indisputable, turn away and seek for refuge in Shakespeare and the musical glasses. I cannot, and if I were twenty years younger I would go about the country and put this simple question incessantly, provided Christian brickbats and hobnails did not murder me, "OF WHAT USE IS CHRISTIANITY?" Say frankly it is dead, that it is an exploded enthusiasm, and I shall respect you. I do not respect hypocrisy either at early communion or in the conventicle.' (July, 1901.)

In a subsequent letter he tries to make his meaning still clearer.

'As to Christianity, you mistake me. I never intended to discuss the general question whether it does good or harm, but I affirm that if we were genuine believers in the Gospels, if we were true disciples of Jesus, not of the official, symbolic, ecclesiastical Christ, but of the real Galilean of Matthew, Mark, Luke and John, we should not be at war in South Africa. . . . Furthermore, that the attempt to reconcile our modern ways with the teaching of the New Testament produces a condition of mind worse than that in which we should be without the New Testament, because we have immorality plus hypocrisy, and because the embrace of opposites is damnation to the soul, incapacitating it for any vision of the truth.'

Mark Rutherford, it will be said, asked too much of his fellow-men. But was it really too much? For remember, he was not asking men to follow 'the real Galilean,' but to be honest and take his name off their banner when they marched to war.

Perhaps, even that is too much to ask; and perhaps, in his despair, Mark Rutherford missed the grain of comfort that is hidden in the fact that though men deny the real Galilean in their acts, they cannot wholly root him out of their hearts nor disown him with their lips. Things have not changed in the twenty-odd years since he wrote; and we have learned a little more from the experience they have brought us. Whether honesty of the sort Mark Rutherford demanded is any more likely to-day, who shall decide? There is COPEC on the one hand, and on the other *The Times* invoking the authority of a Jesuit father in order to confute the COPEC resolution that war is clean contrary to the teaching of Christ. Thou shalt not commit adultery, the venerable straightener explains, is an absolute command; Thou shalt not kill, a counsel of perfection. But why not the other way about?

Yet, obstinate though such questionings were — blank misgivings of a creature moving about in worlds not realized — the cry of irony and despair was not Mark Rutherford's final word.

Far otherwise. He knew deeper than his own painful dilemma. What he knew it would be hard, or even impossible to say. One can do no more than fumble for it through hints and indications: nothing more explicit is to be found in his work, or indeed in the work of any man whom his nature forbids to throw dust into his own eyes. But those who have an ear for the undertones of religious seeking will find much meaning in this confession.

'I will say so much for myself (he wrote to his wife to be on Easter Day, 1908) — that I believe you will find the *truth* in me, and that everything which is vital to you is vital to me, or, in other words, we both live by one Life, which is the Light of the World.

274

This community will come out by degrees. I cannot formulate it. . . . You know that to me the Bible has been from my childhood no mere collection of magic formulas by which to secure safety from eternal punishment. It has been far, far more than it is to the sects and Churches, as I see them. The Jesus-character, I do not mean Christ Himself, is the highest I can conceive possible, but in how few is He really effectual! The whole of Him is not taken and used for the modification of our thoughts and actions; hardly do we take the least part. . . .'

I have no claim to be an authoritative interpreter of Mark Rutherford's religious experience; but I will make this guess, that somewhere in himself he understood why it was impossible for men to follow 'the true Galilean'; and by this understanding I do not mean a mere admission of man's infirmity. I mean far more; I mean a secret and inexpressible comprehension why the ordering of the world must be thus and not otherwise. He could not utter it; no man can. 'What can be shown, cannot be spoken.' But because it could be shown, it was shown, and, by reading the signs and listening for the voice, I am as certain that Mark Rutherford, by his own predestined path, reached this comprehension as I am certain that Shakespeare reached it by his, or Keats by his.

(*June*, 1924.)

275

Quo Warranto?

SOME LITTLE WHILE AGO MR. ALAN Porter, the literary editor of the *Spectator*[1] launched an anathema against this magazine and myself in his leading article. To be accurate, his anathema was levelled less against the magazine than against myself and Mr. D. H. Lawrence. It was a pretty piece of invective, in the main personal. Mr. Lawrence and myself were convicted of dishonesty and vanity, above all of vanity.

'The reason in all of them for all of their misdeeds is a simple and ugly thing. No more, no less than vanity. Vanity causes their individualism, vanity causes their desire to prophesy. Vanity allows them to attack subjects too large for them, and to expatiate with no balance, no strength, no steady fire beneath, giving judgment in a peevish or proud sentence upon a question worthy the deliberation of aeons.'

Then why trouble about us? Works rooted in vanity will quickly wither. Mr. Porter had thought of the simple objection.

'Perhaps it may seem that, beginning in vanity, ending in vanity, their works cannot be dangerous or seductive. But the misery is this . . .'

[1] See the *Spectator*, May 17, 1924.

That, after all, they are seductive. The pity of it!

An indictment for vanity is not worth while repelling. It is too personal to be rebutted without a tinge of self-glorification; therefore it is better left alone.

But, whether or not I am guilty of vanity, it is a bold action in any man publicly to charge another with vanity; a bolder action still to declare, as Mr. Porter declares of me, that all I have written in these pages is rooted in vanity, and corrupted by it.

Whether the charge is true or not I will not attempt to argue. Indeed it cannot be argued, either for or against. My accuser himself does not attempt to argue it. He boldly declares, he gives forth his sentence *ex cathedra*, that I am corrupted by vanity. Before I can accept the sentence I must inquire into the authority of the judge.

Towards the end of his article Mr. Porter himself talks much of 'authority.' He denounces me for rejecting 'authority,' and speaks obscurely of an 'authority' to which 'we must have the clue before we can feel our way to religion.' This misty 'authority' pervades the two final paragraphs of his article; it has neither shape nor name; all that can be definitely said about it is that I reject it, and in its name I am condemned.

Now there are religious authorities which I admit to be authorities, although I do not admit their verdicts as binding upon me. There is the authority of the

Roman Catholic Church, which is vested in the Pope: so far as I am aware it has never been delegated to Mr. Porter. There is the authority of the Established Church of England, which, I believe, resides in the Archbishop of Canterbury, and which, I am sure, has never been entrusted to Mr. Porter. And, no doubt, there are other authorities, whose names and claims are manifest to the world. When we are dealing with them we know with whom we are dealing; if we are condemned by them, we know by whom we are condemned; if we refuse to admit their jurisdiction, we do it open-eyed, with a knowledge of the risk and the punishment. But Mr. Porter's authority is more recondite and tenebrous than these: it has no name, it is simply 'authority.' It can scarcely be his own 'authority' as literary editor of the *Spectator*. That may, for all I know, be considerable with other minds; but it is hardly the kind of authority that can be expected to prevail with me: and to be honest, I do not think this was the authority in whose name Mr. Porter found the courage to hurl 'anathema' at me and all my works.

No, there is an authority somewhere, the nature of which Mr. Porter diligently refrains from disclosing, by which he is empowered to pronounce the verdict 'Guilty of vanity' upon me. I have searched through his article for indications of this 'authority' in order that I might set my own value upon it. It must be a

religious authority, for the grounds upon which I am
condemned are religious. And the only indications
of a religious authority which I can find in his article
are both vague and disturbing.

'There are at present (writes Mr. Porter) curious,
hidden, rather base contributions to our future orthodoxy. Even theosophy, even Rudolf Steiner, even
Gourdjiev, can partly show the path to that self-
deliberation, that utter abandonment of doubt and
restriction, to which Mr. Murry so unconvincingly
lays claim.'

I was not aware by the way, that I had ever made
such a claim. But that is immaterial. What chiefly
interests me is the composition of this 'future orthodoxy,' of which Mr. Porter knows so much that he
can pronounce what are contributions to it and what
are not. That is to say, Mr. Porter has precise and
detailed knowledge of what 'our future orthodoxy' is.
But all the information he vouchsafes to those who
sit in darkness is that theosophy and Rudolf Steiner
and Gourdjiev enter into it – but not D. H. Lawrence
or Middleton Murry.

That, I hasten to say, is no small consolation to me.
I do not like the smell of this 'future orthodoxy': it
smacks too perceptibly of charlatanry and abraca-
dabra and initiation at a guinea a head. But I must
record my astonishment at finding this ambiguous

and subfusc 'religion' the creed of the most conservative of our weekly journals; and it pleases me to imagine the expression in the faces of the country rectors who are reputed to form the majority of the readers of the *Spectator* on the day they wake up to discover that the orthodox religion which it has been inculcating has for its head, not the Archbishop of Canterbury, or even the Pope of Rome, but some unnamed successor to Madame Blavatsky, Rudolf Steiner, and Gourdjiev!

And this 'future orthodoxy,' this vague and shady amalgam of occultism and theosophy and I know not what besides, supplies the authority in whose name I am condemned by the literary editor of the *Spectator*. In the name of such an 'orthodoxy' I am told that 'I must not reject Christianity until I understand it emotionally, rationally, actively.' In other words, I am warned under pain of anathema (duly inflicted upon me) to approach the mystery of Christianity by way of a Blavatsky, a Steiner, a Gourdjiev, or some unnamed other of the same kind, rather than by the guidance of the great men of the past who have helped me to have the courage of my own experience.

But who is the hidden prophet in whom the partial revelations granted to Blavatsky and Steiner and Gourdjiev are made complete? Either he is Mr. Porter himself, or he is some one of his acquaintance; for there is no other means by which he could have this certain knowledge of the 'future orthodoxy' to which each of these approved minor prophets brings his quota. If it is Mr. Porter himself, then he is guilty of dishonesty (which is a greater sin than vanity) in not declaring it; if it is some one of his acquaintance, then he is guilty of a manifest evasion by not publishing his name. I demand to see the signature on the warrant before I obey the arrest.

Let me leave the subject of Mr. Porter and the *Spectator*. I would rather not have dealt with it at all were it not that some simple people have been mystified and troubled by a denunciation so disingenuous. Let me pass to a more important question which might, had my accuser been more aboveboard, have emerged from this debate.

When I am denounced in the name of 'authority,' or in the name of 'tradition,' my instinctive reply is the simple request: 'Show me your authority. Show me your tradition.' There are very few authorities or traditions in spiritual matters, and so far it has invariably proved that those who denounce me in their name do not belong to them. They pretend to be Catholics, they pretend to be Classicists, in order to borrow a bigger stick to beat me with than they can cut themselves. They believe, no doubt, that all's fair in this kind of war. I do not; and I believe that their disingenuousness will recoil upon their own heads. The public which is worth while will in the long run know how to choose between two adversaries, of whom the one puts all his cards out on the table, and the other is occasionally detected with an ace or two from another pack in his sleeve.

In what I have written here I have done my utmost to put all my cards on the table. I have not pretended to believe things I do not believe, or to admire things I do not admire; I have declared my certainties and confessed my doubts. To that extent I am an individualist and I trust I shall remain one till the end of my life. But when I am accused of rejecting authority and ignoring tradition I sometimes feel that I am the only authoritarian and the only traditionalist alive just now. That is, of course, wildly exaggerated. Most traditionalists and most authoritarians, and certainly the best of them, are unconscious of what they are. By force of circumstances I have had to make myself continually and acutely aware of the authority and tradition which I follow; I have been compelled to become a controversialist, and I have to know what my weapons are and where they are. Many of my kind do not know these things; they are not required to know them.

My position is simple. I believe that a man needs both authority and tradition, I also believe that it is best for him to find them out for himself. It may be easier and more comfortable to take them at second-hand; but the easiest way is not the best in the long run. For our longest journeys we choose our oldest shoes; because they are most our own, worn to our feet, and proved by experience. We are fools if we trust to borrowing for those things on which our lives depend. So that for me the question of authority and tradition is quite simply resolved. An authority is one which I discover by experience that I cannot help recognizing as an authority – mysterious words spoken in the past which move my depths and claim my allegiance, even though I cannot say clearly why or how; great imaginations which possess and exalt me, so that I feel moving within them the presence of some truth which I cannot wholly grasp: minds that impress me with a certainty that they possess a deeper knowledge of the mystery of life than any I can claim. These are my authorities, and they are very real authorities to me; very real, because they inspire me with a sense of loyalty to the hidden truth which, I am persuaded, they also served as witnesses and instruments. I cannot give a rational account either of the power of these authorities themselves or of my instinctive recognition of them. They exist, they are part of me, and I try not to betray them.

And these authorities in their long sequence, from Æschylus, Euripides and Plato, through Jesus Christ, through Shakespeare and Keats and Whitman to Tolstoi and Dostoevsky and Tchehov and

Hardy, are the tradition which I acknowledge. I find, when I come to examine them, that all these men of genius, according to the measure of genius that was in them, battled with life for the secret of its mystery; I find that, sometimes in spite of themselves, they were loyal to their own experience. The secret of the mystery was not to be gained by shutting out any part of what they had known or felt; if there was an answer it had to be an answer to everything. I find also that I can trace in all these men who are my authorities and who form my tradition a similar movement of soul: they pass from rebellion to acceptance. That is the simplest and most general statement I can make of their spiritual history, and because it is simple and general it may be misleading. There are as many varieties of experience as there are men; and the shades of meaning in that word 'acceptance' are infinite. Fully to trace the parallels between these hero-authorities of mine, to show the likeness of their struggles and the oneness of their messages, would be the work, not of hours, as this article must be, but of months and years: it is a work I hope to accomplish before I die.

For the moment it must suffice that of this likeness and this oneness I am utterly convinced. To reach this conviction has been a slow and gradual process, and much of the process has been unconscious; much of it, also, has seemed fortuitous. I do not now believe that it was. But at the time it has often seemed a mere accident that I was drawn towards the reading and the study of this or another great man; but once the contact was made a long struggle has begun. For me this struggle to comprehend has never been a dilettante affair or an intellectual exercise. I make a poor showing as a dilettante, and intellectual exercises for their own sake have always left me cold. To me the effort to understand has been almost a matter of life and death. Some chance-read word has engaged my soul, and I have felt that the man who spoke it had some message of infinite import for my life. I have gone blindly on, saturating myself in what he said, until at the last I have been satisfied that I know both what he meant and what he was. And sometimes I have not merely been satisfied; I have been certain. I have been given proof that I understood.

I will give an instance, not to glorify myself – indeed, there can be little glory in revealing how I am convinced by proofs which to many men would be fantastic – but in order to show, if it can be shown, the order of knowledge on which my attitude to authority and tradition is builded.

But first I must give the background of belief against which my small discoveries are made. I believe that there is a final truth and an ultimate wisdom, and that it is achieved by those heroes of humanity who have battled with life in loneliness. This final truth and ultimate wisdom cannot be declared; it is by nature unutterable, save by parable and symbol and art. The most naked revelation of this truth and wisdom which has been vouchsafed to the Western world is in the words and the life of Christ. Those words and that life are not to be easily understood; but the deeper our own experience of life descends and the more loyally we abide by our experience, the more intimately we understand the words and life of Christ and the more profound is the illumination we receive from them. They become for us the supreme type, the symbolic mystery of human experience. That is not, by its own very nature cannot be, a dogmatic certitude which can be communicated to, or implanted in us at the beginning; it can only grow slowly within us, it can be ratified only by our own experience, as we find the movement of soul and the symbolic tragedy of Christ repeated in our other hero-authorities. Thus I have learned that Shakespeare can only be comprehended by reference to this archetype of the individual soul. I find that the tragedy of Shakespeare as it develops becomes more and more a declaration of triumph in disaster: the defeat of goodness and nobility in *Lear* and *Antony and Cleopatra* is not accounted for by any defect in the goodness and nobility which suffers defeat. Aristotle's rational explanation of tragedy is left behind; we have entered a realm where it no longer has validity; we are, in Shakespeare's hands, being steadily led to a point at which goodness suffers catastrophe, simply and solely because it is good. That to Aristotle was a 'monstrous' conception. Three hundred and fifty years later that 'monstrous' conception was to be proclaimed as the ultimate truth of life by the symbolic tragedy of Christ, and in this sign a new epoch of the human spirit was to begin. This final monstrous tragedy, to which Shakespeare was being driven, he did not write: he touches the verge of it, he shows us that it is imminent and necessary – and he gives up writing tragedies altogether. He has touched the unutterable mystery, and he turns away from the Kingdom of Earth to the Kingdom of Heaven. He imagines a generation which shall be born with the vision and the knowledge he has worn out his life in achieving, and he spends his latter years dreamily declaring, through the figures of Perdita and Marina and Miranda, the truth he knows: 'Except ye be born again, ye shall in no wise enter into the Kingdom of Heaven.'

When great spirits touch a certain depth of knowledge of human life, this is the path they follow – the path that leads to a new comprehension of the mystery of Christ. When in a writer's work I am thrilled by contact with this depth of knowledge of human life, I am certain that I shall find him at the last fol-

lowing this predestined path. Such a profound depth
of knowledge I found in Herman Melville's *Moby
Dick* — knowledge of the same order that is in *Lear*
and *Macbeth*. The end, I said to myself, will be the
same. At that time I could not prove it. Melville's
later works are rare, and two years back they were
impossible for me to obtain. I had to bide my time
until a few months ago when four supplementary
volumes to the collected edition of Melville's works
were published — volumes which contained the un-
procurable and 'unintelligible' works of his long
period of silence. I turned to the last of these, an
unpublished story, written with pains and care,
immediately before his death — his final word, his
spiritual testament. It contained precisely what I had
expected: a deliberate effort to restate the mystery of
Christ — the catastrophe of the utterly pure and good,
and its complete triumph in the very moment of
death.

That for me was proof enough; but it happened
that I wanted something more. I knew that Melville
had read, had truly read, Shakespeare. In his curious,
reticent, self-suppressed essay on Nathaniel Haw-
thorne, he confesses to a deep knowledge and admiration of Shakespeare. I wanted more than that : thousands of people confess as much, and give not an
inkling that they know what Shakespeare really contains. But I who was certain now that I understood

Melville, was also certain that he muſt have underſtood Shakespeare in the same way as I underſtood
Shakespeare (more profoundly in that same way, of
course, but in that same way). Somewhere, somehow, I felt, Melville muſt have left behind him a
word telling what Shakespeare truly was to him. If I
could find that my laſt doubt would be gone. One
day, as I was reading through his odd and ungainly
poems, fascinating only to those who know Melville
well, but to them immeasurably fascinating, I lighted
— with what a thrill of excitement! — upon a short
poem about a picture of Hamlet. All the surround-
ing poems were battle-pieces ſternly lamenting the
heroisms and horrors of the American Civil War: in
their company it seemed at firſt absolutely irrelevant.
It was absolutely relevant; for this is what it said:

> 'No utter surprise can come to him
>   Who pierces Shakespeare's core:
>   *That which we seek and shun is there —*
>   *Man's final lore.*'

'Man's final lore.' That was my final proof.

I have chosen this inſtance of Shakespeare and Melville because it is the lateſt of a long sequence of such
inſtances. These heroes of mine, as I come to comprehend them, become my authorities and form my
tradition. They are not authorities who can be acquired at second-hand, nor do they form a tradition

which can be learned by rote: neither can they be
used as a club to bludgeon my opponents. And,
again, — and this is important — they are not anyone's
private property: access to them is free to any man
of good will, provided that he be himself free, *nullius
addictus jurare in verba magistri*. Not one of my
authorities commands credulity: not one commands
anything. But with one voice they say: If you listen,
we will speak; if you try to understand the mystery
which even we could not declare, it will be revealed
to you. We seek from you no submission but that
which you, of your own soul's motion, cannot refrain
from giving. We also were rebellious, and we know
that only he who has rebelled can accept.

When I am pursued as a heretic in the name of a
dubious 'authority' and an unformulated 'tradition'
and 'a future orthodoxy,' when I am charged with
overweening vanity simply because I believe, and say
I believe, that the only authority and tradition which
will truly support a man are the authority and tradition he discovers by his own effort to supply his own
need, — then I make my request: 'Show me your
authority. Show me your tradition.' My accusers
do not show them to me. Do they think that I shall
be frightened by the mere word Authority with a
capital A or Tradition with a capital T? I do not
believe they do. But they think they will be able to
frighten people more credulous than I am, or give

some façade of superior understanding to those who would like a comfortable excuse for neglecting this magazine.

But though my accusers do not show me their tradition and their authority, I have not hesitated to show them mine. I have not the least desire to over-awe them by it, or even to show them that they are wrong in supposing that I put myself forward as a prophet without authority or tradition to impose my *ipse dixit* on the world. If they really believe that, it is certain that even this article will not convince them to the contrary. I merely wish to compel them, if I can, to emulate my example, and to declare the nature of their authority as honestly as I have declared the nature of mine.

(*July,* 1924.)

Lost Secrets

SOME TIME AGO, ATTEMPTING TO describe the religion of Mark Rutherford, I touched on the fringe of a question which seemed to me at the moment of such importance that I must put it away for the time. I had the sense that I was on the verge of a realization into which I could not wholly enter; I was excited and troubled by the presence of a thought to which I could give no form. I could not grapple with it; so I gave it hurried words which might serve, as a rough sketch in a painter's notebook, to recall it to me later, or at least to remind me that here was a door I must one day try to open, a road I must explore. In the meantime, if I were to let the thought fall back into the darkness from which I had half-lifted it, it might, when next I tried to raise it, have taken a shape of its own.

There are those, I know, who hold that if a thought or perception is not expressed, it is not a thought or perception at all. In a sense this is true. A thought which eludes expression is certainly not a complete thought; it has not attained to full being. But, on the other hand, it is not nothing. It is not yet communicable, and therefore it is without value to the world: it is not yet an object. Nevertheless, it is something, and something precious to the mind which is aware of it. Though it is without form, we know it is not void: and that is nearly all we do know.

But that knowledge, and what is known by it, are not nothing. The famous philosophy which declares that they are nothing, is wrong; it misses the truth, falsifies the reality, by its own excessive schematism. These unfledged thoughts are very real to the person who is troubled by them; and if the reality they possess for him is not reality according to the philosopher's scheme, that only proves (what in his heart everybody knows) that there is more than one kind of reality for our limited human minds. Such surmises as I am trying to describe have a very acute personal reality; they seem to beckon, to call to us imperiously, imploringly, desperately: 'We have a secret for you: if you do not wrestle with us for it now, it will be lost for ever.' And very often they call to us when we cannot pause to question them, because we are intent upon another goal, and we have to stop our ears against their foreboding cry: 'We are important, and what you are seeking is not important at all. The end of your journey is with us, and not whither you are hurrying.' But we feel that if we stopped to listen, the journey's end would never be reached. Whither we are bound, we are certain of arriving; but if we were to listen to the Siren voices, we should have nothing done by nightfall. We say this to ourselves and hasten on; but we do not really believe these were Siren voices — the note was one of anguish, not of alluring sweetness — and when we have passed them by our hearts are heavy as lead, and their despair is ours. A sense of doom descends upon us: we have denied a god, the secret has indeed been lost for ever.

Lost secrets are like lost causes. Though the philosopher and the man of common sense may agree that they are nothings, they haunt men's minds and compel their loyalty. The philosopher may declare that 'the light that never was on land or sea' is not a light at all, and the man of common sense may demand what earthly good such an illumination can be; we may agree with the one, that it is indeed not a light, and with the other that it is of no earthly use, and still have the conviction that it is something more than a light, and of considerable heavenly use, if we could but make it ours. Nor is it utterly futile if our half-possession of it never becomes whole. To be convinced that a secret is there, even though we may fumble in vain all our lives for the key, is to be of a different mind, perhaps even of a different kind, from those who believe that there are no secrets unless they are revealed.

Therefore, the despairing sense that a secret has been lost for ever is not altogether despair; it brings with it an acknowledgment that we are of one kind rather than another, and such acknowledgments are good. And even when, having been driven by a sort of remorse to turn back along the road we came, we stand and stare at the marks we made to remember the place where the voices called us, our own blank amazement that we could have believed that these contradictory signs would point to the treasure changes into a truer wonder that signs so crude could have signified so much. That, at least, was a minor miracle, and we were the witnesses.

So it is but half in despair, and half in wonder, that I stare at the words I wrote – even strictly, the marks I made – two months ago when I was hastening along a road that should lead me to an understanding of Mark Rutherford's religion. The marks are these: –

'And sometimes lately I have thought (though it may be an impossible dream) that what the world is waiting for is union in the awareness and worship of the God who is ineffable. If men could only be content to allow what their liturgies describe as ineffable – unspeakable and therefore unspoken – something would have happened to the mind and soul of man: they would be changed, and that change would mark a new epoch in the history of the spirit of man.'

That is all; yet when I wrote it, it meant much. It was a pointer to a thought I could not comprehend. I knew perfectly well that it did not express the thought, but I could not forgo making the mark.

Perhaps it would help me to remember when the time came to wrestle with it.

The time has come. I stare at the marks and try to remember. I remember all manner of things I had forgotten: where I sat at the moment the half-thought came to me, and at what hour – in the window-seat of a bedroom overlooking the village street in the late afternoon, while I was talking to a friend. It seems to me now that had I not been talking, I might have made it my own: so my friend was like Coleridge's 'person from Porlock,' but I have no Kubla Khan to show. And then it seems to me that had I not been talking, I might not have had even the half-thought, for it arose out of conversation. I try to remember what I said.

I was talking about what I called the mistake of formulation. I felt that the formulation of God held men back from a sense of the reality for which the word stands. The old Jewish name, with its peremptory rejection of all formulation, as limiting the majesty of the divine, was the profoundest the human mind had yet devised – I AM THAT I AM. If we could hold a sense of the meaning of that name, and know it not as an impassable barrier, but as a direct road to the central mystery, the human mind would be changed, and there would be the beginnings of a new relation between men. For, I said, a change in this consciousness of ours is surely imminent, for it is necessary: we have worn it out. It has led us to a point at which the next step seems to demand the annihilation of the mind that brought us there. Either a new *kind* of comprehension will begin, or the human mind will begin to devour itself, as indeed it seems to have begun. Nevertheless, I believe that something else is also beginning, which might be more plainly manifest if men could join together on the basis of that which they do not formulate. That would be a new relation, for men have hitherto been joined on the basis of that which has been formulated. But this relation, I said, is almost impossible to express in words, for our words belong to the old mind, and we are demanding that they shall express the new. That, and I believe no other, is the reason why what I have said sounds at first like a mere negation — a union between men on the basis of what they do not do. But it is *not* a negation: just as I AM THAT I AM is not a negation, but the most terribly positive affirmation of the knowledge of God that has ever been made. Just as that name is a paradox, so any name for the relation between men I dimly conceive, which might come to pass under the sign of that name, would also be a paradox. This union would not be a union; it would be rather a diversity: but more truly still it would be a new positive relation, and that is why a paradox is necessary even to hint at it.

So far my mind had carried me – I am remember-
ing truly now – when the half-thought came. Now I
no longer spoke. And this new sense of the reality of
God will come (I thought), this new relation between
man will begin, when we have passed beyond the
greatest and the most insuperable of all our formulations – the formulation into life and death. It is this
which holds us back. We formulate truly into life
and death, and then we deny one of the terms of our
formulation, we rebel against death: we strive to overcome death, by striving to believe in personal immortality. But this is not to overcome death; it is to
falsify death, it is to try, vainly, to change death into
life. But life and death are real, and true opposites.
To try to change one of these opposites into the other
is to make one of those true opposites false, and to
make null and void the opposition which is true. The
kingdom of life cannot be extended over death; and
not only can this not be done, but the attempt to do
it wears the human soul away in vain. The pain and
darkness of death are not lessened, the regret for life
is not diminished, by this despairing effort to believe
in a personal immortality. What is diminished is the
majesty and co-equality of death; the great reality of
death is denied. It is not that a belief in personal
immortality is a cowardly thing – no living man has
the right to call another a coward before death –
but that it prevents men from taking a step forward

which would free them from the fear of death for ever.

If they would recognize the majesty of death and its co-equality with life — neither the one nor the other more splendid, more necessary, nor more true; neither death the plaything of life, as those who would believe in personal immortality make it, nor life the plaything of death, as those make it who suffer their minds to prey upon their souls — then surely we should see that life and death, in their magnificent opposition, *must* be a formulation of that which is beyond them, and is one. It is the outworn consciousness which drives men on — in ever more futile and pitiful forms — to deny the fact of death The prying spiritualism, the muck-raking of eternity, into which even men of science have lately fallen in a degradation of human dignity; and the instinctive nobility of the human soul turns away from it in pity and disgust. In our hearts we know better than that; we know how to choose between these sordid affronts to the majesty of an event that fills us with awe and wonder, and Walt Whitman's co-equal song: —

'Come, lovely and soothing death,
  Undulate round the world, serenely arriving, arriving,
  In the day, in the night, to all, to each,
  Sooner or later delicate death.

Praised be the fathomless universe,
For life and joy, and for objects and knowledge
    curious,
And for love, sweet love – but praise! praise! praise!
For the sure-enwinding arms of cool-enfolding
    death.'

Surely we know which of these is true, and which holds out to us the promise of enduring comfort.

To deny death is to deny life, for these two are bound together in an equal bond. Not to acknowledge death profoundly and in the depths of one's being, not to have felt the glory of its substantial mystery, is not to acknowledge life nor to have felt the solemn splendour of its inscrutability. And not to have felt these comrade mysteries for what they are is to be deprived of the vision of the great mystery which they hide and reveal. Behind them, and in them, is the ineffable Life of which they are the manifestations. In that Life, if we may dare to call it Life, life and death are reconciled and one; and we humans, in so far as we in ourselves truly reconcile life and death, diminishing nothing of them, acknowledging them for what they are, knowing that each of them is greater than ourselves and not to be measured by the rod of our understanding or desire, can reach an awareness of that which includes them both. Life and death are our ultimates, set in a true opposition,

which is not a condition of hostility, but one of recip-
rocal necessity. When we know that our ultimates
are thus opposed, we know also that there is beyond
them that which is greater than they are, yet can be
comprehended only through them.

Of this greater thing we can *say* nothing; we cannot
even name it, save by such a nameless name as the
Jews of old gave to the unspeakable God: I AM THAT
I AM. This ineffable Life and that ineffable God are
one. Though we cannot name this One, we can be
aware of it, we can know it. As yet our knowledge can
be only fitful and momentary. Could we but make
it permanent and abiding, the nature of our consciousness would indeed be changed, for we should
know all that we know as a visible shadow of the
manifest mystery we should steadily comprehend.
We should not look, as we do, from outside a veil,
through the veil, to that which is concealed within,
but we should look with a single act of vision both
at what is concealed and at the veil which conceals.
With one glance we should see the reality and the
necessary symbol of the reality; we should behold the
One as it were flowering into the opposites under
which alone we can contemplate it now; we should
know that what is must be thus and not otherwise,
and also know that neither we nor the created universe suffers compulsion; we should be free of the
limitation, against which we now chafe in vain, by

which we are compelled to divide the one kingdom into a realm of necessity and a realm of freedom, for we should understand the necessity that these two realms should be; we should know yet more — we should know the nature of true Necessity and how it includes those opposites under which we are as yet compelled to apprehend it — freedom and necessity. At every point where the knowing mind is baulked by the rampart of some secular antinomy and falls back wearily upon itself, there would be a passing beyond, if the lust of formulation could once be truly relinquished.

But this true relinquishment must be quite other than a mere fatigued letting-go of the knowledge we have. It is not by ceasing to regard any of the great opposites as real that we shall overcome their oppositions; it is only by admitting their reality more fully than men, save only a few, have dared to realize them that we shall attain to a positive comprehension of that which is through and in them. To hold the great opposites together, in our minds and in our souls, as of equal truth and equal potency, to stand fast by *all* our knowledge, however contradictory it may seem — is the road to victory.

Of all the great oppositions, the opposition between life and death is the one that sits closest to us; moreover, it includes the others, because all that we may be, and therefore all that we may know, depends upon our attitude to this. If men could overcome death, not by falsely representing it as life, but by accepting it for what it is — 'Death is life's high meed' — their inheritance in life would be changed. They would be free to be and to know; they would not be fevered by a sense of futility, nor overwrought by impatience to achieve. If they could resolve this opposition, they would resolve all oppositions, not only because they would have reached to a knowledge of the ineffable Life in which all oppositions are included, but because their souls would be calm and fit to look steadily at the oppositions which remain. For the new knowledge will be rooted in a state of soul. We must be in order that we may know.

This is the deepest paradox of all. To achieve the state of soul in which true knowledge is possible, we need to have achieved the knowledge. We must be in order that we may know, and we must know in order that we may be. Yet, paradox though it is and must be, it is not insuperable. Our new and true knowledge can come to us at first only in gleams. If we hold fast to these, the calm will come in moments also; in those moments of calm, we shall catch a fuller gleam: and so, from fuller gleam to longer calm, the slow conquest will proceed, till our knowledge is an abiding possession and an enduring peace is in our souls.

Let us begin, then, where we must begin: let our credo be not only 'I believe in life,' but also and

303

equally, 'I believe in death.' If we can truly believe in these two majesties, we shall have won no little way towards a belief in that which gives them both their sovereignty. And this belief will not be the belief of faith; it will be the belief of knowledge. To hold in the mind and soul life as it is and death as it is: that is all. To that knowledge all knowledge will be added. But we, who have believed in life too glibly, as Europe has always believed, must begin with death. We have to know death in order to know life.

After all, this is not new. Our men of vision have always told us this. Shakespeare's voice rings out with Whitman's in a triumph song to death. We can, if we will, follow every moment in the deep adjustment of his soul to the reality of death, from the moment when in *Measure for Measure* he begins to wrestle with the dark angel, gazing with fear and fascination into his eyes, to the moment when in *Macbeth* the dark wings have cast their shadow over the whole of life, on to the moment when in *Antony and Cleopatra* life and death become equal and equally acknowledged royalties. ' I will be,' cries Antony,

'A bridegroom in my death, and run into it
    As to a lover's bed.'

And Cleopatra echoes him: —

'The stroke of death is a lover's pinch
    That hurts and is desired.'

304

Beyond that moment in Shakespeare, when he reached 'the top of sovereignty' and envisaged opposites 'all calm,' comes the moment of full knowledge, the comprehension of the ineffable, which not even the greatest artist can represent, though he may see, face to face.

So, in being remembered, my half-thought grew to this; but only half-thoughts still, and not more than half-expressed. But even so a gleam which to one man brings a calm, which may in turn be visited by a fuller gleam.

Religion and Christianity : a Reply

BY THE REV. W. E. ORCHARD, D.D.

BOTH THE RELIGIOUS AND THE LIT-
erary public are in considerable debt to Mr.
Murry for having published his article on 'Religion
and Christianity.' He has broken through that
tradition of reserve on religious matters on which we
English sometimes pride ourselves, but which, as a
matter of fact, constitutes a very serious deprivation
to our knowledge and understanding of religious
matters. It is a momentous thing when a man becomes sure of God, and it is a great service to his
fellows both to confess it and to tell them how he has
become sure. But while Mr. Murry has been frank
about his own religious certainty, the position which
he has gained has led him to a somewhat astonished
discovery, namely, that ordinary Christians do not
share his assurance, but build their faith on a quite
different basis; and he sees in this the cause of so
much of the inefficiency of the Church and the lack of
practical power in the faith of so many ordinary
believers. Following on from that discovery, he
comes to the conclusion that the orthodox Christian
faith has gravely misinterpreted Christ, indeed, has
completely transformed His message and meaning,
and that the Christian Church is founded not on a

positive and personal experience of God, but actually in order to supply its lack.

Mr. Murry has very courteously asked me to criticize his article from the general Christian and Catholic point of view. I am not sure that I am competent to do so, and it is an unwelcome task to criticize a religious experience which has obviously brought to the writer such strength and peace; and not one word shall be said that casts any doubt upon its reality or power. It is only in so far as this experience is turned into a criticism of the orthodox Christian attitude towards faith and its assurance that I should dare to say anything. But there one must be as frank as Mr. Murry himself has been, because great issues are involved for other believers, however different their experience or the basis on which their faith rests.

Mr. Murry's discovery of the difference between his own experience and that of other professedly religious people was made through conversations that he has had with Roman Catholics and Anglicans. He has evidently been telling them how and why he believes in God and explaining that with him it is not belief so much as knowledge, for he declares he is as sure of God as he is of the existence of the outside world. But just because he is so sure of God, he wonders how anyone else can believe in the dogmas of the Christian Church. An eminent Roman Catholic, with whom Mr. Murry raised this question, replied that there was no difficulty in believing in the dogmas of the Church if once you believed in the existence of God; it was that which was the difficulty; and when Mr. Murry replied, 'But I *know* that God exists,' his Roman Catholic friend answered: 'You're lucky.' At once the whole situation was revealed to him and the difference between believing dogmas about God and knowing God immediately for oneself was made clear. He says, 'I find it inevitable to believe in the existence of God and impossible for that very reason to believe in dogma.' Dogmas would never be needed at all, indeed they would appear irrelevant, if one really knew God; therefore he concludes that ecclesiastical dogma rests on an entirely different basis from personal faith. Moreover, another thing immediately became clear to him, namely, that Catholics make so much of the Church because they are afraid of standing alone; they are not personally sure about the fundamental thing, namely, God, and therefore they club together in the hope that this uncertainty will be compensated for by the faith that can be gained from fellowship and that rests on authority. Mr. Murry thinks that the man who believes in God does not need a Church; if you find God as a self-discovered certainty you are willing to stand absolutely alone.

It is obvious that Mr. Murry has not quite understood the Catholic position. I should like to have overheard that eminent Catholic saying, 'You're lucky,' for I should have needed to catch the tone of his voice to know whether he was crediting Mr. Murry with a genuine mystical experience, or whether he was questioning whether Mr. Murry really knew God as certainly as he thought. It was probably the combination of an assurance of God as a reality as certain as the existence of the external world, together with a complete perplexity concerning the need of dogmas and of a Church which probably prompted this somewhat ambiguous, not to say rather flippant, remark; but concerning the inner meaning of that conversation we shall probably have to remain in the dark; although I think if Mr. Murry could persuade the eminent Roman Catholic to give *his* interpretation of the conversation, he would do us all a great service. But in default of that, it would perhaps be worth while for the readers of Mr. Murry's article to give some thought to the general Catholic philosophy concerning belief, faith, and knowledge. It can be stated roughly somewhat as follows: belief that God exists can be gained from the data delivered by the intellect considering the phenomena of the external world. If anyone thinks about these things and asks the question how the world came to be his intellect will lead him to the conclusion that there must be a God. That conclusion will never be in the nature of an absolute demonstration; such a thing is in the circumstances impossible; but the certainty of God's existence will put that man under grave moral responsibility unless he goes on to seek for faith, which is a gift of illumination bestowed as a reward for a sincere acceptance of the position to which one's thought has led, and this will be a humble petition for that which shall bring assurance. This faith, when given, brings an assurance not only that God is, but of what He is, what His attitude towards man is, what He is willing to do for man, and so ultimately, step by step, to an acceptance of the whole Christian system, including the dogmas embraced by the Creeds and the authority claimed by the Church. These dogmas and the Church's authority are not claimed to be rationally deducible from the fundamental fact of the existence of God: such doctrines as the Incarnation and the Trinity are based on what is called Revelation, that is statements made by such persons as prophets, apostles, and pre-eminently by Christ, which are delivered by them with the conscious claim that they are speaking in the name of God, and are invested with a peculiar solemnity which brings to the mind a feeling of inspiration, or authority, or an immediate response. But although they could never have been discovered by Reason working unaided, they are now seen to be not incompatible with Reason. Moreover, when carefully considered, they alone give a basis to Reason itself, to its universality, to its power and its trustworthiness.

But in addition to this gift of faith there may come to the soul, through the practice of prayer, gradually, or by some sudden illumination, a sense of God which seems to be immediate, overwhelming and brings an assurance the soul cannot possibly doubt; this is believed to be a foretaste of the final condition of the soul, only perfectly attained in the other world, when God will be directly apprehended by the soul as clearly and gloriously as the sun is seen by the eyes. It is not denied that this mystical consciousness of God comes to people in many different ways and may be found apart from the Church and its Sacraments, and, indeed, outside Christianity altogether. But it would also be held that while this gave a great assurance, it would often be lacking in two important particulars; first it would be bound to be rather inarticulate; if a man were asked what God felt like, or who was this God of whom he was so sure, he would be unable to say; he would only know *that* God was, but he might not be able to say *what* He was, Secondly, it is just conceivable that under the pressure of the crude facts of life, the suggestions of scepticism, and the perhaps temporary cessation of this assurance, a man might wonder if after all the experience was true, and to make up for these deficiencies he would have to turn to Reason, to ecclesiastical dogma and to the experience of the saints to confirm and establish his assurance.

Now Mr. Murry's certainty about God is obviously of this mystical type, and has both these defects. It is at least remarkable that never once in his whole article does he tell us what he means by God. He does not need to, he knows what he means; but does anyone else know what he means? How can he assure anyone else that it is not just a feeling of his ideal self, or the cosmic consciousness, or the unity of all life, or any other vague thing which has been identified with God? It may be that Mr. Murry will yet one day look back upon this undoubted experience and doubt whether it was real, and he will then want to turn to something else for help.

It is not perhaps surprising that in a vague theological conversation these matters were not all made clear, but Mr. Murry might have been aware that terms were being bandied about which need a somewhat careful definition; for instance, knowledge is a very ambiguous word, and may mean either an immediate consciousness of a thing, as, for instance, when we say that we know of the existence of anything; or, it might mean knowledge of a person sufficient to recognize that person, or perhaps such an intimate knowledge that we might even presume to say that we knew how he would act in a given circumstance; or, knowledge might stand for a scientific demonftration; the complete explanation and analysis of some existing thing. A line of Tennyson's ought to have come to his mind, and would have been sufficient to put him on his guard:

'We have but faith, we cannot know,
    For knowledge is of things we see;

which quite rightly implies that our knowledge of God is not the same thing as the demonstrated knowledge of science; though it might also be claimed that faith brings a much higher assurance of things that cannot be seen than science can ever give us of things we do see. Mr. Murry is confusing *certainty* with *knowledge*; for while certainty may be felt by any one of us beyond the possibility of doubt, this can hardly be called knowledge unless it can be shared by others and can be shown to be true. Now strangely enough he tells us that 'God need not be defined, because He does not need to be shared.'

Perhaps sufficient has been said to show that the Catholic philosophy has at least got a place for Mr. Murry's certainty, but it would never dream of building everything on that alone. It ought to be remembered also that if anyone is asked suddenly about the nature of his religious faith the immediate answer and the language employed need to be judged very carefully. If I were asked if I was as sure of God as of the outside world, I should certainly hesitate; for while I am sure of the outside world I have never met with any proof of its existence; and my assurance of God is so different that I cannot really compare the two things.

But it is serious that on this basis of certainty Mr. Murry should feel it necessary to deny the Divinity of Christ, and to decry the value of the Church; for while his vision of faith may not move any unbeliever nearer to belief, it might move a good many people away from Christ and the Church without any corresponding gain in mystical assurance. Mr. Murry has already most courteously and frankly acknowledged to me that the ascription of fear as the foundation and bond of the Church was a hasty assumption and may be taken to be withdrawn. But something does need to be said to counteract the statement. When I read that Catholics do not claim to know God, and that they join the Church simply to overcome the uncertainties which they dare not face, there leapt into my mind literally scores of names. Did St. Paul know nothing of God when he sought Baptism? Were the hermits of the Thebaid, St. Theresa and St. John of the Cross persons who were afraid to venture out into utter loneliness and desolation of soul in order to become absolutely sure of God? Did Pascal, who was an intellectual sceptic of the most penetrating type, not know it when he wrote of his experience: 'Certainty, Certainty, Certainty,' and yet did he not seek the fellowship of the Church and join the community of Port Royal? Mr. Murry uses more than once the word 'luminous' in order to describe his own state of belief, and the very word recalled some famous words: 'I rest in the thought of two and two only supreme and luminously self-evident beings, myself and my Creator.' These words were written by a cardinal of the Roman Church, John Henry Newman!

It is the more astonishing since God has become so really clear and necessary to Mr. Murry's thought that the value of Christ to him should consist solely in the fact that He was a man. I hesitate again to criticize Mr. Murry here, because he has entered so closely into the message of Jesus and His call to men to cease to rest upon anything this world can give and to venture all upon God; and yet to adopt this purely humanitarian conception of Christ means to ignore many of Christ's own words and some of the most fundamental things in His own consciousness. Surely Catholic dogma would have been a little help to Mr. Murry here, for it does affirm Christ is truly man, but also that He is God: God and Man. Therefore I simply fail to follow the distinction that if Christ is man we are bound to follow Him, whereas if He is God we cannot. This is a common modern confusion that Christ's work for man was to provide him with a human example: it was rather with an example of Divinity, to which we are actually called. If Christ is not divine He cannot lift us to Divinity, and He then tells us no more than the prophets of Israel or the seers of Paganism, and He does not meet the need of mind or heart. It seems so strange that Christ should be worthless if He is God, when it is God of whom Mr. Murry is so sure and from whom he derives such strength. And it is not perhaps unfounded to suspect that on analysis he would find his idea of God has been derived from Christ, not only as a teacher, but as an actual revealer, and the image of God.

That leads to another question, whether after all Mr. Murry is quite so independent of reasonings as he claims to be. It is difficult to believe that his assurance of God, whether it came gradually or suddenly, had nothing to do with previous intellectual work and that he had not been arguing with himself along rational lines. Can he also be certain that the Church has had nothing to do with it? He has a theory of Christ's meaning on which he must reject as a sheer invention on the part of the Church a vast amount of the Gospels, but it is still to these Gospels he must appeal to support him; that is, he has to appeal to the Church's own documents. But would he know anything about Christ's attitude towards God and His message to humanity if there had been no Church to transmit even that knowledge? It is more than unlikely. He seems to have fallen into one of the commonest errors of modern criticism which first assumes an authority which it afterwards denies. Unfortunately Mr. Murry may find sufficient evidence all down the ages of the Church's unfaithfulness to Christ, and he is probably right when he says that you cannot expect a body to move as individuals can; but it is surely a daring and unwarranted conclusion that this unfaithfulness is due to the fact that Christ has been regarded not as human, but as divine, and that He has been made 'the God of a Church instead of the example of a man' in order to evade His obvious demands. It is a tremendous work, of course, to make anyone faithful to Christ, and we may admire and love Christ long before we come to that; and it is a still greater task to lift any organized body of people to a level of faithfulness; but we shall certainly not lift them any the sooner by saying that Christ was only human. And Christianity has no practical message for this world unless it can offer some hope that an organization can also be lifted into faithfulness, even though the process may be slow. Why some of us are so concerned about faith in the Church is not because we are afraid, but because if there is no hope of Christ's Body, the Church, at length corresponding to its Divine Head, we can see little hope of the redemption of humanity. And if the Church has utterly failed, then Christ has failed too.

But He Himself declared that there would be in the Church examples of failure because of the human and evil elements gathered into it; but nevertheless, that its failure would never be the final fact about it.

It may be said finally that Mr. Murry's article does nevertheless serve to emphasize the fact that the institutional element in religion is always in danger of the means being made the end; but that does not imply that the mystical element can stand alone or that even God can redeem the world apart from an organization. And it is unbecoming to souls who have climbed as high as mystical assurance to grow contemptuous of the steps by which others must advance. There is something about this type of thought which is not only individualistic and unChristian, but irreligious; and the judgment which it often passes on people beneath it, or on the Church as a whole, is painfully reminiscent of Pharisaism. No one can dispute that the very existence of the Church, its creeds and its Sacraments are the outcome of mysticism; that they demand mystical vision for their understanding and comprehension; and that it is mystical experience which the whole aims to produce. Again, in Catholic popular theology the humanity of Christ is certainly often overshadowed. But to declare that Christ is God and not man is a heresy: Christ's human experience is a real one and His human life was lived in order to show how we could live in perfect dependence upon God. But despite all the failure that can be blamed against the Church and individual Christians, there is no sort of proof that those who deny Christ's Divinity have followed Him more nearly than those who accept it: the humanitarian conception of Christ may often produce a very upright and philanthropic life, but very rarely does it lead to the heroic sacrifice and self-negation which the Catholic system has always been able to produce. The life to which Christ calls us is a supernatural life; no doubt when this is realized it enables scores of Christians to plead off anything but the most far-off following of Christ; but excuse and evasion are not to be confused with the effects of a real understanding of that utter humility and condescension which the Incarnation declares to be the very essence of God; for it is this which has converted sinners and created saints. The Incarnation is a necessity if we are going to be certain that our assurance of God is not a mere interior delusion; we must see God also coming to us in an objective historical person; we must have something to answer modern doubt when it suggests that God is after all merely our deified self, or some phantasy of the mind which we have created in order to console ourselves for our own failures. If it be true that sometimes popular Catholicism has overlooked the necessity for leading people from a merely accepted authority to a personal experience, it must be remembered that Catholicism has produced the greatest quantity of mystical experience, while the mysticism outside this system, the existence and value of which Catholicism has never denied, has often lost itself in the deserts of subjectivism and individualism, only to end in doubt and selfishness. The Catholic philosophy of faith has room for Mr. Murry's experience and gives to it a very honoured and valuable place, but it is the only philosophy that provides it with an adequate explanation, saves it from delusion, and can gather together and channel the power of such an experience so that it is available for all mankind and is preserved intact across the centuries.